Destiny is a word we don't use much anymore. It implies some set fate to which we are inexorably drawn, even if it goes counter to our conscious will and intentions. These days we prefer to think we have more freedom of choice.

But we have to acknowledge that in many respects our lives do seem to be determined by influences beyond consciousness.

This book is about becoming aware—aware of how you can alter your patterns of expression and become the very best you can be. It is particularly oriented toward joining the art of astrology to the art of tapping the subconscious mind. Whether you are an expert or a complete novice in the field of astrology, you will learn how to increase your potential for meaningful self-expression by activating deep personal resources and rechanneling negative expressions of cosmic energies into positive ones.

—from the Introduction

Changing
Your
Destiny

CHANGING YOUR DESTINY

Dynamic New Astrological and Visualization Tools to Shape Your Future

Mary Orser and Richard A. Zarro

1817

Harper & Row, Publishers, San Francisco
New York, Grand Rapids, Philadelphia, St. Louis
London, Singapore, Sydney, Tokyo, Toronto

The authors gratefully acknowledge the following sources for permission to reprint brief passages:

Astrology Beyond Ego, published by Quest Books, Wheaton, IL. © 1986 by Tim Lyons. *The Global Brain: Speculations on the Evolutionary Leap to Planetary Consciousness* by Peter Russell, © 1983 by Peter Russell, reprinted by permission of Jeremy P. Tarcher, Inc., Los Angeles. *Peak Performance: Mental Training Techniques of the World's Greatest Athletes* by Charles A. Garfield with Hal Zina Bennett, © 1984 by Charles A. Garfield, reprinted by permission of Jeremy P. Tarcher, Inc., Los Angeles. Excerpts from *The I Ching Workbook* by R. L. Wing. Copyright © 1979 by Immedia. Reprinted by permission of Doubleday, a division of Bantam, Doubleday, Dell Publishing Group, Inc. "Research Affirms Power of Positive Thinking" by Daniel Goleman, *New York Times*, February 3, 1987, copyright © 1987 by The New York Times Company. Reprinted by permission. *The Presence of the Past: Morphic Resonance and the Habits of Nature* by Rupert Sheldrake, © 1988 by A. Rupert Sheldrake, reprinted by permission of Times Books, a division of Random House, Inc. *As Above, So Below* by Alan Oken, © 1973 by Bantam Books, Inc. *The Horoscope: The Road and Its Travelers* by Alan Oken, © 1974 by Alan Oken. *Mysticism and the New Physics* by Michael Talbot, © 1980 by Michael Talbot. From *Beyond the Quantum* by Michael Talbot. Copyright © 1986 by Michael Talbot. Reprinted with permission of Macmillan Publishing Company.

FIRST EDITION

Designed by Irene Imfeld

Library of Congress Cataloging-in-Publication Data

Orser, Mary.
    Changing your destiny.

    Includes bibliographies.
    1. Astrology.   2. Self-realization—Miscellanea.
3. Visualization—Miscellanea. I. Zarro, Richard A.
II. Title.
BF1729.S38077 1989   133.5   89-45238
ISBN 0-06-250675-7

---

89 90 91 92 93   10 9 8 7 6 5 4 3 2 1

Richard A. Zarro dedicates this book to his family: his parents, Eugene and Vita, who taught him the power of love, persistence, and faith; his brother, Ronald, for his brilliant research and constant support; his daughter, Hope, a miracle child, who is the joy of his life and living proof of the existence of heaven.

Mary Orser dedicates this book to all those starwise people who have helped us know the universe and to all those change agents who are working for a transformed world.

CONTENTS

1. Activating Your Astrological Potential   1

We can guide, in positive directions, the manner in which our lives reflect patterns in the heavens.

2. Why Does Astrology Work?   15

New scientific understanding shows the interrelation of physical, biological, and consciousness fields with their contents.

3. The Enchanted Mind   35

You, a spirit, direct your holographic information and retrieval system through the power of attention and visualization.

4. Relaxing Your Way to Full Potential   57

Self-guided imagery can change not only your view of reality but also actual events.

5. The Transforming Zodiac   75

The twelve phases of the cosmic cycle are expressed in basic, universal themes.

ILLUSTRATIONS

Preface:
Dancing on
the Omega Point

Everywhere on Earth, at this moment,
in the new spiritual atmosphere . . . there float, in a state of
extreme mutual sensitivity, love of God and faith in the world:
the two essential components of Ultrahuman.
These two components are everywhere "in the air" . . .
Sooner or later there will be a chain-reaction.
TEILHARD DE CHARDIN

✳

This is an extraordinary and exciting time to be alive. This is the time of miracles and wonder that has been promised us through the ages. Ancient prophecies are being fulfilled; esoteric secrets are being made simple. In astrological terms this is the Age of Aquarius, a golden age of peace and spiritual enlightenment.

It is a time of great transformation, both personal and global. Now, with the emergence of new understandings and new technologies in the fields of science, psychology, and spirituality, it is possible for everyone to achieve states of excellence and peak performance that were previously reserved only for the few—and for those few only after years of study and practice. Now, many people are reaching states of excellence in a short period of time, even in endeavors that once seemed beyond reach.

For example, until several years ago firewalking was the secret ability of the priests of Bali or the monks of Tibet. To participants it was magic. Now, for a little money and an evening of their time, over fifty thousand people in the United States from all walks of life have learned to walk on coals registered at 2000° Fahrenheit. As the science fiction writer Robert Heinlein said, "One man's magic is another man's engineering."

This new engineering gives us a powerful technology with which to shape our future and that of the world. It is possible to achieve states of enlightenment—self-transformational states—without years of practice in an Eastern or Western monastery. If we can have instantaneous destruction on this planet, then we can also have instantaneous enlightenment.

We have the knowledge and technology to take care of the basic needs of everyone on the planet. It is a matter of *doing* what we already know how to do. For instance, we produce more than enough food to feed us all—and it would be possible to organize its transportation and distribution so that everyone could be fed. When enough of us visualize and work toward a world in which everyone eats, such a world will come about.

The encouraging factor is that more and more people are paying attention and acting as if "We Are the World," changing their own lives and thus becoming, for themselves and others, transformers, "change agents," as Peter Russell calls them. "Think globally, act locally."

A radical and rapid shift of life as we know it is taking place on this planet whether we like it or not. Either we will learn to love and care for the planet, ourselves, and one another, or we will destroy our life through any one of a dozen doomsday scenarios that the media warns us about—ranging from being burned to a crisp by the ever-increasing hole in the ozone layer to the new plague of AIDS. Either we will learn to forgive and help one another, or we will destroy one another. Brutality has become commonplace and appears on evening television as entertainment and news, both in personal lives and in the fifty-seven wars going on in 1989 on this planet. People who are afraid together create disasters together. (*Disaster* originally meant a "negative star," and this book is about turning negative stars into positive stars.) But the energy that has been expressed in destruction can be turned to construction, the conflict turned to cooperation in creating a better world.

We must and will tap into deeper resources if we want to survive. Because of the various crises on this planet and the monumental decisions we face within the next decade, the prophesied transformation must take place. It is our spiritual inheritance.

And there are tools now available to help bring about that awakening of our hearts and minds, to help us be the very best we can be. The universe's gift to you is who you are; your gift back to God's universe is what you become.

＊

In this book we will be presenting you with some of these tools, but first some personal notes from each of us as to how this book came about.

Richard: I have had the pleasure of knowing Mary Orser for fifteen years. Her national reputation in astrology is well deserved—she has written four books on the subject and helped develop the Astrodeck, a card deck that explains astrology. She has given thousands of personal readings and dozens of seminars, and appeared on radio and prime time television (the David Susskind Show). She is on the leading edge of astrological thought. Her educational credentials include a Bachelor of Journalism from the University of Texas and Master of Arts in psychology from the New School for Social Research.

Mary is one of the most congruent people I know. She lives her beliefs in such a manner that people seek her out as a model on which to base their lives. A vegetarian for over forty years, she looks and moves like a young woman. Many are surprised to find that she is sixty-four years old. Her house is simple, exquisite, with stone floors and beamed ceilings, far up a mountainside in the Catskills. Her life is wonderfully balanced between deep spiritual practice and service to the world through the astrological metaphor, helping an inestimable number of people achieve more productive and satisfying lives spiritually and materially.

It was a great honor for me when she asked if she could attend the seven Futureshaping Technologies™ seminars I gave to train the staff of Omega Institute in Rhinebeck, N. Y.—a New Age center that has recently achieved international status and acceptance in such divergent and unexpected "mainstream" publications as *Fortune* magazine.

Mary was a witness to the profound changes brought about in the fifty students over a seven-week period as they assimilated the Futureshaping technology and applied it to their lives. I also noticed a sudden brightening of her eyes and nods of her head as I explained my unified field theory of hypnosis called Holographic

Hypnosis™ and Holographic N.L.P., incorporating a unique combination of quantum physics, zen, lucid dreaming, Neuro-Linguistic Programming (N.L.P.), Ericksonian hypnosis, Dr. Sheldrake's M-field, Dr. Lovelock's Gaia hypothesis, Dr. Pribram's holographic mind theory, and the unlimited potential that is the power we call love.

Mary and I decided to have a meeting to discuss how these breakthroughs in Futureshaping techniques were connected with the breakthroughs in understanding astrology that are being brought about by the same exciting theories.

Mary: Astrology is one of those fields of knowledge that have many levels of understanding, each more exciting and enlightening than the last. As I have journeyed down and up these levels, I have increasingly seen the power of this art and science to throw light on our lives and to transform them. But understanding is one thing—making the transformations is another.

I was somewhat familiar with a number of consciousness-changing techniques, such as meditation, visualization, and self-hypnosis. I had seen these practices bring some important life changes both to myself and to others. Also, I had heard that Richard's techniques were easily learned and highly effective for helping people perceive and tap into their deep personal resources and potentials, far beyond what they had ever thought possible. People had been drawn from all over the United States and Europe to his seminars and private intensives.

Therefore, I was delighted with the opportunity to see in action Richard's wonderfully dynamic synthesis and expression of the art of consciousness-changing. When I attended the Futureshaping Technologies™ seminars at Omega Institute, I was impressed by what I saw and experienced. Richard had put together a dynamic set of techniques that were able to bring amazing breakthroughs. Moreover, he could explain why these techniques worked in the context of the new scientific breakthroughs. The same tools that have helped thousands achieve their personal state of excellence are introduced to you in later chapters of this book.

That day in Richard's Japanese garden, he was telling me about techniques for bringing about states of excellence that can only be described as self-transformation. I was telling him about how the new science is putting astrology back into a meaningful context. From earliest times people have used the Sun, Moon, planets, and stars for navigating not only on their journeys over land and sea, but also in the courses of their lives, whether they were leading nations or simply charting personal directions.

This book came about because we saw that joining the art and science of astrology to the art and science of transformation makes it possible to achieve states of excellence in expressing astrological potential that most of us have touched only rarely.

TRANSFORMING

No matter what technology or set of tools you choose to change your destiny or fulfill it, if it is not done with love, you have not tuned into the entire purpose of this mysterious and marvelous journey we call life.

We are born at a certain astrological time, determining certain holographic events that we will face. And life is the guru, the teacher. Life is patient—if we don't get it right the first time, the event will be repeated. These repeats we know as patterns in our life's expression. There is no priest, preacher, mystic, guru, or monk who has God's unlisted number. If anyone hands you that line, they are trying to pull a fast one on you.

Dr. Ronald Zarro says in his lectures: "God has an 800 number. You can dial direct. The age of gurus is over. Just spell the word guru out loud, *Gee* yo*U* a*Re* yo*U*. Trust yourself. Dial God direct."

Isms, and ologies are just tools, like the ones you'll find in this book: relaxation techniques, visualizations, powerful astrological metaphors. Try them out, take what works for you, and leave the rest behind. Then use your personal set of tools to enhance yourself, making your life more fun, more exciting, more prosperous spiritually and materially. In doing so, the lives of all those connected to you will be enhanced. They will begin to love themselves and trust themselves more, as you have done, and the people around them will also be affected by this positive flow, and it will go on and on, changing the entire world.

You are much more powerful than you realize. Later in this book we will describe the new insights into fields, especially Dr. Rupert Sheldrake's M-field theory. You will begin to understand how every little change you make in all aspects of *your* life also changes the world in ways previously thought impossible.

Donald Keys, in his book *Earth at Omega*, said,

> This is not to assert that all persons need to
> become saints, spiritual adepts . . . for humanity
> to survive; although given the heat and the pres-

sure of today's circumstances, it is quite likely that these times will produce more than the usual quota of graduate humans. What we will need to avoid catastrophe is a critical mass of people—and ultimately of nations—who have adopted good will as their dominant expression in personal and international affairs. . . . We each have a task to be more aware, more whole. Our role is in helping heal humanity. We each need to become conscious cooperators and good stewards, no longer estranged from each other but more aligned with the pulse of life's planetary purpose.

Becoming more conscious and aligned with the pulse of your astrological gifts can help you along that path.

Peter Russell, in *The Global Brain*, said:

The transformation of society awaits the transformation of the self—of enough selves, at least—to tip the balance. What we need for planetary emergence is the next appropriate step for each person. When the transformed seeker becomes a knower, then he or she becomes a powerful force for human unification. The very being of such a person manifests it, telegraphs it, radiates it throughout the global network of subtle human connectedness and . . . will elevate the whole . . . each person will be a midwife to the most amazing event of human history: the birth of the global entity.

It is then that the prophecies of the ancient astrologers about the dawning of the enlightened, golden age of peace and prosperity, the Age of Aquarius, will be fulfilled.

"Remember," said the Mother of the Sri Aurobindo Ashram in India, "that you are at an exceptional hour in a unique epoch, that you have this great happiness, this invaluable privilege, of being present at the birth of a new world."

May each of us carry this spiritual mandate, the destiny of our generation, with exceptional grace.

ACKNOWLEDGMENTS

The creation of this book was a team effort. We would like to give special acknowledgment to:

> John Grinder, Judith DeLozier, and Associates for the excellence and magic of their N.L.P. training seminars and personal guidance. Special thanks for developing this fabulous technology.

> Michael Talbot, for his inspirational conversations and provocative books.

> John Anthony West, who shared his research for the revised edition of *The Case for Astrology* (which he wrote with Jan Toonder), to be published in 1990.

> Scott Siegel, our agent, for his quiet persistence and belief in the project.

> Mark Salzwedel, for his vision and guidance.

> Peter Blum, for his expert editing and advice.

> Sheryl Stewart, for her loving care and renewal.

> Carol McDonald, for her early dedication to this book when it was only an idea.

> Catherine Sklarsky, for her thoughtful and intuitive research into astrological mythology.

> Marian Tortorella, for her knowledgeable compiling of attributes and affinities of the zodiac signs and planets.

> Carol Marks, for long-term faith and guidance.

> Megan Denver, for her computer work and emotional support.

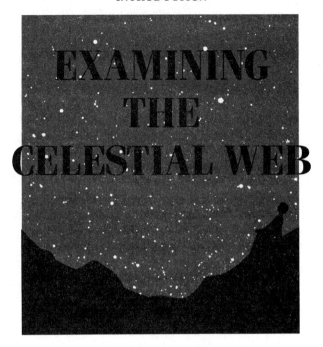

EXAMINING THE CELESTIAL WEB

The horoscope is a blueprint of our character.
Character IS destiny. There is nothing static in the universe
in which we dwell. We can change by changing our
attitudes and patterns of behavior. In so doing, we change
our destiny.... The stars impel but do not compel.

Man is not what he is because he was born when he
was. He was born when he was because he was
potentially what he is.

ISABEL HICKEY, *Astrology, a Cosmic Science*

❋

Destiny. *The end to which all unrestrained forces lead.*
The aim of most religions, including Astrology, is to help one
to become the master of his Destiny. Lacking this mastery,
Destiny largely determines the part we play in the
scheme of things. Destiny vs. Will adds up to experience,

*as a result of which we can be said to evolve, and become a
developed or remain an undeveloped child of Destiny.*

NICHOLAS DEVORE, *Encyclopedia of Astrology*

✴

Destiny is a word we don't use much anymore. It implies some set
fate to which we are inexorably drawn, even if it goes counter to
our conscious will and intentions. These days we prefer to think
we have more freedom of choice.

But we have to acknowledge that in many respects our lives do
seem to be determined by influences beyond consciousness.

This book is about becoming aware—aware of how you can alter
your patterns of expression and become the very best you can be.
It is particularly oriented toward joining the art of astrology to the
art of tapping the subconscious mind. Whether you are an expert or
a complete novice in the field of astrology, you will learn how to
increase your potential for meaningful self-expression by activating deep personal resources and rechanneling negative expressions
of cosmic energies into positive ones. You will also find that the
same techniques can be used to transform negative expressions of
your energies in other ways.

We live in a time of tremendous breakthroughs in understanding how our universe works and how we are connected with it.
These developments on the leading edge of knowledge show that,
in many respects, the universe we live in is spectacularly different
from what we had thought. Investigators in various areas of study
are realizing that the characteristics of matter, the forms of living
beings, the very events of our lives are intricately connected to a
variety of fields that fundamentally determine what goes on
within them.

We are familiar with such physical fields as the force around a
magnet or the gravitational pull of the Earth, but recent work also
shows the importance of other and much larger fields of the physical universe, and new kinds of fields with quite unusual properties.
Besides fields in particular areas, there are nonlocal fields for which
distance is no barrier. For example, nonlocal biological fields have
been suggested, fields for each species. Among birds, for instance,
there might be such a field guiding the development of the egg into
the adult and programming behavior such as courtship and nest
building. No matter where a warbler might be located, it might
always be tuned to and influenced by the warbler field.

And, even more fascinating, consciousness fields are being pictured: archetypal (overarching) fields that influence both how we perceive our reality and how we act. The zodiac signs, planets, and other astrological factors can be seen as powerful archetypal fields.

It is also becoming clear that there are feedback loops between the field and the particulars within it (atomic particles, objects, persons, planets, etc.): *As the field influences what happens, what happens modifies the field.*

There have been major breakthroughs in understanding *why* reality manifests itself the way it does and *how* to change the way the multiple available realities manifest themselves. Astonishing advances have been made in the art of tapping the subconscious mind in ways that can reprogram patterns that formerly seemed beyond our control, thus, in a sense, changing—transforming—our destiny.

In chapters 3 and 4 we will be describing these discoveries and giving you techniques for applying them to make changes you may not have dreamed possible.

STAR PATTERNS AND DESTINY

For centuries people in many cultures have seen a relationship between personal destiny and patterns formed by the Sun, Moon, planets, and stars. In our Western culture this study—astrology—became separated from the mainstream of scientific studies beginning around the seventeenth century. The scientific explanation of the mechanics of the universe that was popular at that time could not explain why astrology works. By the eighteenth century the "general attitude of the time seemed to be one of complete scepticism in regard to the possibility of divination through the stars."[1]

In the twentieth century, however, the breakthroughs mentioned earlier are helping us understand the universe from an entirely different perspective. A theoretical framework has emerged that is beginning to explain how the patterns of the universe relate to the patterns of our lives on Earth. We are understanding, for instance, that one of the many fields influencing us is the field of our solar system. We resonate with the electromagnetic field associated with the continually changing pattern of Sun, Moon, and planets. And it seems that the *solar system is also a consciousness field*—we resonate to its changing moods, we dance to the music of the spheres.

In chapter 2 you will learn more about this new framework for why astrology works. It opens many doors, one of which brings us to a place where astrology is again becoming acceptable as a valid and valuable field of knowledge about our world. This, of course, means astrology as a science and art, not the newspaper zodiac column parody of it.

From the beginning of recorded time until recent centuries astrology was seen as important to many other fields of knowledge. Since it went out of favor in halls of learning around the time of Newton (although he, himself, accepted it), astrology has been treated with respect by very few people in the sciences, although thinkers in other fields have occasionally recognized it. For instance, Ralph Waldo Emerson said, "Astrology is astronomy brought to Earth and applied to the affairs of men."[2] John Burroughs put it: "Man is a little piece of earth, with a little piece of sky over him; and all the laws of this outward earth and sky are repeated in him."[3]

In our times astrology has been especially frowned upon—something not to be taken seriously. This was hilariously evident in 1988 when it was revealed that President and Mrs. Reagan had been consulting an astrologer to determine affairs of the government of the United States. Most commentary in the news media either ridiculed the whole thing or expressed fear that, if the judgment of our country's leader was so off that he actually listened to an astrologer, no one could tell what other lapses of judgment he might have.

It was not always so. Several of the Founding Fathers practiced astrology, including, of course, Benjamin Franklin, whose *Poor Richard's Almanac* gave detailed astrological data.

From Washington on, several presidents are known to have consulted astrologers, although they have not all generally admitted it. Theodore Roosevelt, however, said of his horoscope: "I always keep my weather-eye on the opposition of my Seventh House Moon to my First House Mars." This not only reveals that he had some detailed knowledge of his horoscope, but also that he understood it to some extent and kept track of present influences.

In 1963 a number of astrologers saw that some intense connections were coming up between the current pattern of the planets and the planet pattern when President Kennedy had been born—his horoscope. One way in which this combination of patterns could be played out might result in his death. Astrologer Jeanne Dixon tried to get a warning to him, but in the parallel universe we are living in, his life did not change course, and he ran aground.

We will be talking more about parallel universes later, because not only is this concept being considered by physicists as a possible way to explain phenomena in the *material* world, it is also a meaningful way to visualize what can happen in our *consciousness* and in the flow of events. Basically, the parallel universe theory says that "for each of us, an indefinite number of universes exist simultaneously. Each universe may be a slight variation of the next one or may be entirely unrelated."[4]

The intense planetary pattern of that day in Dallas as combined with President Kennedy's horoscope could conceivably have been played out in many ways. A theme that would have been constant for that time is some kind of death, and death always implies a new birth. In one parallel universe he goes to the funeral of someone he loved. In another he abandons a course of action for carrying out his policies and begins to make other plans.

In a parallel universe nearer the one we were in, he narrowly escapes the bullets in Dallas. The impact of this near-death experience begins a spiritual rebirth for him that brings great wisdom. He leads the country into a flowering of its highest potentials. The United States becomes a model—the ideal government for serving its people, for giving them the freedom to pursue their own highest goals. The people are brought to a state of unity in which the country leads the world in improving the quality of life on Earth.

Throughout this book we will be giving you tools for accessing alternate parallel universes for expressing your astrological patterns.

PURPOSE

This book has two major aims. The first is to show you how to recognize the possibilities for expressing various astrological themes. Our second aim is to show you how to visualize, harmonize, and actualize them—to make your life a fulfilling expression of celestial (and other) themes.

Throughout this book we will be coming at you from two different directions: on one hand, *what* astrology can tell you and what working with that knowledge can do for you; on the other hand, *how* to do it—techniques for successfully releasing astrological and other kinds of personal potential.

We are also approaching you from another pair of angles:

Understanding how things work: Part of the time we will focus on information about what has been learned and what can be accomplished, as well as techniques for doing it. We will give you data, evidence, theories that tie things together, as well as "how to" hints—what can be called "left-brain input."

Visualizations, the "right-brain inputs," are aimed at giving you the experience of what we have been talking about—putting you into the picture you have been looking at. Chapters often start with a visualization (in **bold**) related to the chapter subject.

As you progress through our book, you will first see only the broad outline. Then the picture acquires perspective and detail until, when you finish, you can see the mental hologram three-dimensional and alive.

NOTES

1. Serge Hutin, *History of Astrology* (New York: Pyramid, 1972).
2. Quoted by Alan Oken in *As Above, So Below* (New York: Bantam, 1973), 27.
3. John Burroughs in *Under the Apple Trees* (Boston: Houghton Mifflin, 1916), 133.
4. Bob Toben and Fred Alan Wolf, *Space-Time, and Beyond* (New York: E. P. Dutton, 1975), 25.

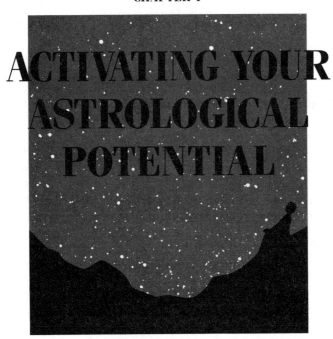

CHAPTER 1

ACTIVATING YOUR ASTROLOGICAL POTENTIAL

A physician without a knowledge of astrology has no right to call himself a physician. . . . There is one common flow, one common breathing, all things are in sympathy.

HIPPOCRATES, FIFTH CENTURY B.C.

Astrology is assured of recognition from psychology, without further restrictions, because astrology represents the summation of all the psychological knowledge of antiquity.

C. G. JUNG

The purpose of . . . astro-psychology is to help the person to actualize innate potential, to bring what is only possible to an at least relatively complete state of fulfillment.

DANE RUDHYAR

✳

Imagine this ... You are standing in the center of a small circle of tuning forks, one for each note in the musical scale. They are ordered by pitch, so that when you turn around the circle one way, striking each tuning fork as you face it, you are going up the scale, and when you turn around the other way, you are going down the scale.

Surrounding this circle, some distance away but still within hearing, is a larger circle of tuning forks arranged in the same order as your inner circle. A person is walking at a steady pace around this larger circle, striking every tuning fork in turn. You are aware that each tuning fork in your little circle vibrates when the corresponding pitch is sounded in the outer circle.

Now you see that there are a number of other people—smaller people—also going around the outer circle. Each of them is moving at a different speed, ranging from very fast to so slow that you can barely see their movements. They, too, sound each tuning fork as they pass, although usually not as loudly as the first person.

Resonating on your small circle of tuning forks, you can hear the changing music made by the outer circle, chords formed by the continually altered combination of tuning forks being struck. Sometimes these chords are more harmonious, and sometimes more discordant, but you sense that even the most dissonant chords are resolved in their higher harmonics.

You find yourself dancing to this music—sometimes lightly and playfully, sometimes heavily and dramatically, with a rich variety of moods in between. Sometimes your dance is joyful and flowing, and sometimes you are greatly challenged to create a dance that expresses the beauty of the discordant passages.

You see that each person in the outer circle is giving off light, and each is carrying a big prism. As their lights bounce off each other's prisms and are reflected to you, you are bathed in a continually changing play of colors.

*

Now you stand on a small mountain at the center of a circular continent. Radiating spokes divide the continent like a wheel, into twelve territories. From your hub you can see into all twelve territories, but the light is clearer in some of them, and these are the ones you are more focused on.

Each territory has a very distinct personality with a particular terrain, climate, soil, rocks, plants. Each is distinguished by the

2

colors and sounds, the kinds of birds and fish and animals it con-tains. The people of each territory are as distinct as their environ-ment. They have characteristic appearances, customs, ways of doing things. Different things are important to them.

Three of the territories produce people who serve the continent by sparking enthusiasm—the adventurers, inspiring leaders, phi-losophers.

Three other territories produce those who work with the earth, building; the practical scientists and engineers, people who get things done.

Another three territories have people who focus on networking, communicating, trade, weighing matters, contacting others.

The final three territories are home base for people who tune into the feeling side of life—those who nurture others, who play with the harmonics of the dance of life, who dream.

∗

In the first visualization you may have understood that the outer circle of tuning forks represents the big circle in the sky that we call the zodiac, and that the people going around the circumfer-ence are the Sun, Moon, and planets. The big person is the Sun. The inner circle is the pattern of your horoscope.

In the second image, you began to get acquainted with the quali-ties of the zodiac signs.

All of the bodies in our solar system appear to travel along the same zodiac path as they circle us in the sky. The pattern that they form in the heavens around us, the *macrocosm*, is reflected in our individual lives, the *microcosm*.

> It is the same One Force expressing itself in an infinite multitude of forms and intensities. This is often called the process of "Involution and Evo-lution." It is also what we mean, in part, when we refer to the universal law of "As above, so below." Just as an atom is one unto itself, so is Man such a singular organism, so is a nation, so is the Earth, so is the Solar System, so is the Galaxy, so is the ultimate Universe of Universes. In all of creation there appears to be a repetition of the same pat-tern in all structures from the physical properties of the tiniest atom to the greatest unit of the

Cosmos. Thus the macrocosm (the greater world) is always seen as revealed in the microcosm (the lesser world). This is what is meant when it is said that "man was made in the image of God."

ALAN OKEN, *As Above, So Below*

PATTERNS IN THE HEAVENS AND IN OUR LIVES

These visualizations are one way to understand what astrology is: the study of patterns in the heavens as reflected in events and in patterns of behavior on Earth. It is an ancient art and science, practiced in many cultures through the ages, because it has helped human beings understand and predict the characteristics of different times. This is because the changing patterns made by the Sun, Moon, planets, and stars have been found by astrologers to symbolize the characteristics of the time period.

We can think of these patterns of interrelationship among heavenly bodies as cosmic chords in the music of the spheres, like background music in a theatrical performance.

But, and this is important to understand, the changing cosmic music (like theater background music) indicates only the themes of the time. These themes can be expressed by a variety of specific actions and events.

In this book you will learn techniques that can reprogram your subconscious mind so that astrological energies that had been negatively expressed are rechanneled into self-fulfilling powers. As Elisabeth Haich said in *Initiation*, "There are no bad energies, only energies which are badly used."

The particular cosmic chord that was resonating at the time you were born—your horoscope—can be considered a holographic imprint that conditions your ways of expressing yourself. (We will talk more about holograms later.) During your lifetime you play out themes and variations expressing the characteristics of this imprinted cosmic chord. This is where our freedom of action comes in: Although all of us express, in one way or another, both our imprinted individual horoscopes and the present planet pattern, these patterns can be played out in an amazing variety of ways, ranging from catastrophic to peak performance accessing unlimited potentials and resources.

4

YOUR HOROSCOPE

What can your horoscope tell you about yourself?

The word *horoscope* is from the Greek *horo*, hour, and *skopos*, watcher. It has come to mean the map of the sky as it appeared from the birthplace at the moment of birth of an individual or at any other significant moment. You are pretty sure to know one feature of your map—the zodiac sign the sun was in when you were born. (See the notes at the end of chapter 5 for these dates.) As seen from the Earth, the Sun goes through each sign at approximately the same time each year.

The ancients observed that, as mentioned earlier, the Sun, Moon, and planets all appear to circle the Earth along a relatively narrow background pattern of fixed stars. In different countries and different ages a variety of names have been given to the sectors of the sky through which this highway passes. Our Western culture calls the sky highway the *zodiac* (from the same root as *zoo*), meaning "a band of animals," and we divide it into twelve sectors called *signs*, most of which bear the name of an animal that seems to characterize the sign. The division of the zodiac into twelve parts is found in a number of other cultures, including the Chinese, which also names the signs after animals.

Sky watchers have found that people born at the time the Sun passes through a particular section of this band seem to show similar characteristics. The Sun is the only celestial body that is seen to travel around this vast circle exactly once a year. The Moon and planets are on the same road, but their speeds are different. The Moon circles the zodiac once a month, and each planet completes the cycle in a different length of time, ranging from less than a year for Mercury and Venus to 248 years for Pluto, the outermost known planet. Therefore, the zodiac positions of the Moon and planets do not have to be the same as the Sun sign at any given time.

The Sun, Moon, and each planet have been found to symbolize different functions in your life: the Sun your consciousness and will, the Moon your subconscious, instinctual reactions, Mercury your thinking and communications, and so on. The zodiac sign each planet was in when you were born seems to modify the expression of the planet. It has been likened to a glass filter that colors the light shining through it from the planet. Thus, a person born when Mercury (signifying thinking and communication) was in Taurus (patient, practical, deliberate) naturally develops com-

5

munication patterns that express Taurus characteristics. For example, he or she may focus more on practical matters and reach decisions slowly.*

Getting acquainted with each zodiac sign's basic symbolic characteristics as well as its more frequent manifestations is something like getting to know the people of a certain nationality—you begin to recognize the spirit of their culture at the same time you are learning some of their more frequent idiosyncrasies. You begin to see how quite different individuals express similar cultural themes—or similar astrological themes.

What signs were the Sun, Moon, and each planet in when you were born? Which signs and planets are emphasized in your horoscope? If you have had your horoscope made, this information is available to you. If you have not, see the last page of this book for where to get an inexpensive and accurate computer horoscope that will give you this information.

In addition to the zodiac signs, we will describe key characteristics for each planet. Putting together your understanding of the planet–sign combinations can help you understand some of the self-fulfilling potentials that can be developed with these energies.

The sky map of your birth has many other features, the study of which can greatly enrich your understanding of the potentials of your cosmic birth imprints. We will help you find and understand these features—without having to make calculations or learn complex astrological techniques.

The main thrust of this book, however, is not to confuse you with the complexities of astrology but to give you tools for transforming your negatively expressed astrological patterns into positive ones, using new Futureshaping Technologies™ based on relaxation and visualization.

DEEP POWER SOURCES

In all cultures it has been recognized that when an individual or group manifests real power, that power wells up from the depths of the psyche rather than from conscious or unconscious superficial motivations. People who have accomplished the most, either as individuals or as charismatic leaders, have tapped into the strong

---

* (Most astrologers work from an Earth-centered viewpoint because you were born on Earth. If an astronaut should give birth to a baby on Mars, we would set up a Mars-centered horoscope.)

stream of these deep power sources of the subconscious. In fact, most of us have had the experience of thinking we couldn't accomplish something and then sensing a welling up of energy that enabled us to do it with surprising ease. It is as if we suddenly connected with far more horsepower, like the famous second wind of marathon runners.

Being able to reach deep power sources can greatly increase our potential for living in a creative, satisfying, and spiritually harmonious manner. This incredible potential can manifest itself in many ways. Compulsions, addictions, and obsessions are also manifestations of power from the inner psyche, often going against the conscious will.

The ancients called these power sources "the gods." The word *enthusiasm* originally meant "possessed by a god." Our grandparents might say "the devil got into him" or "an angel helped her."

Modern psychologists have referred to some of these energies as *instinctive drives, collective patterns, archetypes,* and so on. We can think of them as dynamic patterns on various subconscious levels. Each of us is tuning into, resonating with, many patterns, which range from a manner of walking or gesturing to the strongest archetypes, such as the hero or the great mother. The more universal archetypes have been symbolized in many ways, but over and over again certain themes—seemingly basic to human nature—have stood out.

Astrology is a symbolic system that expresses these basic themes. As Karen Hamaker-Zondag has said:

> The signs of the Zodiac, the planets, houses, etc. can be rediscovered in everyone's psyche; they are Archetypes which have assumed definite forms, representatives of psychic material and processes which man has learned to cope with through the long centuries.[1]

When the archetypes in our collective unconscious—including those of astrology—are activated in our personal lives, this tremendous power is going to be expressed in one manner or another. But these expressions can take myriad forms, both powerfully destructive and powerfully creative. This book is about rechanneling the energies of astrological archetypes in ways that can greatly enrich your life.

Just how we express the imprint of these cosmic factors is a matter of conditioning. We are programmed in many ways: by our culture, family influences, and personal experiences, which the mind stores and holds as belief systems. For example, if we have heard or read about how cosmic influences are supposed to affect us, that belief can influence us, as it did the Aries child we will tell you about below.

But, as mentioned above, astrological patterns are, in themselves, neither positive nor negative. The problems and potentials of these patterns depend on *how we react* to them. (See chapter 3 for more about this.) In other words, the basic qualities of the imprinted cosmic chord that accompanies our lives may be considered fated, but we have some control over what kind of dance we do to this music. This is a how-to book for learning to respond to your basic imprints in a creative and self-fulfilling manner.

For example, let us say that the zodiac sign Aries is strongly featured in your horoscope. (Later on we will tell you what makes a sign "strongly featured.") In essence, Aries energy is characterized by showing enthusiasm, initiating action, going in new and unique directions, and expressing individuality.

Aries energy is positively manifested in the exploring and pioneering of new territory, knowledge, and ways of artistic expression, as well as strong self-expression and acting against resistant patterns—people and situations that impede a dynamic flow. However, the negative cultural habits associated with Aries include being foolhardy, going off half-cocked, fighting, having a "me-first" attitude, and insensitivity to the needs of others.

In addition to the influences of your culture, you can also pick up negative habits from your immediate environment, especially early home experiences. Astrologers have long noted that emphasis on certain zodiac signs runs in families. It is very likely that at least one person in your family has a horoscope with strong focus on a sign or signs that are featured in your horoscope. Just as we pick up from our early environment physical mannerisms and speech patterns, so also we acquire habits that express our horoscopes. If Uncle Harry demonstrated the strong Aries side of his nature by continually fighting to get his own way, then your own Aries nature undoubtedly picked up a few pointers.

Even beyond such influences, we are conditioned by the personal habits we develop. If Aries is strong in your horoscope, you may have expressed this from early childhood by being impulsive and adventurous, supercompetitive, quick to get excited if thwarted. As soon as you learned to crawl, your mother had to be on the alert to grab you by the diaper as you headed rapidly and fearlessly out the door, into the street, or to reach for that beautiful flickering flame.

You probably did not take kindly to this interruption of your forward momentum, especially if she reinforced it by telling you that you lacked caution and had a terrible temper. So you may have built up an identification with such negative Aries traits, seeing yourself as somebody who regularly gets mad and can't control potentially harmful impulses.

Aries emphasis will always incline you to get started and move faster than most people; your emotions will be more volatile, and you will strongly focus on your individual self-expression. But all of these characteristics are powerfully positive in the right context. In this book you will learn to recognize the malfunctions of each sign as well as the self-fulfilling potentials that are possible when the energies are rightly expressed; you'll learn, as it were, to make lemons into lemonade.

OTHER ASTROLOGICAL FACTORS

As mentioned, in addition to the zodiac signs, certain planets are emphasized in your horoscope. These, too, have a variety of modes of expression. They are like the inhabitants of the zodiac territory, the facets that make up your personality. Saturn, for example, has been found to relate to the structuring of your life, your awareness of cause and effect, your responsibility. A negative Saturn expression is the tendency to be so cautious that you won't make a move if there is any possible doubt of the outcome. This, of course, boxes you in and destroys spontaneity. When your Saturn energy is functioning in balance, you can be cautious where it is appropriate and spontaneous where that is called for. The chapters on each planet will tell you more about this.

Besides the zodiac signs and planets, there are other important astrological factors. These include what are called *aspects*—the patterns formed by the relationship of the planets in the circle of your horoscope—and the horoscope *houses*.

In later chapters you will learn about positive expressions of aspects and houses, and how these combine with the planets and zodiac signs to create more inspired potentials of the moment you were born, and therefore of yourself.

Here is an example of how the planet pattern of a certain date can be expressed in very different ways: The horoscope of the day the atomic bomb was dropped on Hiroshima is extremely intense. Its patterns indicate the *bringing to light of deep inner power and the sudden breakthrough of energies*. This, of course, was expressed clearly by the bringing to light (public consciousness) of the deep inner power of the atom through the sudden explosion of its energies.

We have the horoscope of a woman born in the United States on the same date. She bears the imprint of that day and its intensity. She is an extraordinarily powerful personality, a psychologist who, in helping her patients, is particularly focused on the use of startling techniques to *bring to consciousness deep inner power by the sudden release of restricted energies*. She is using in a very positive manner the themes of the day that were so catastrophically expressed by the atomic bomb.

Besides working with your birth horoscope, you will also learn how to determine what present and future astrological patterns can tell you about the territory you are traveling through—helping you avoid pitfalls and realize the potentials of the changing qualities of the times.

HOW TO UNLOCK POTENTIALS

To reprogram your unconscious habits of misusing an astrological imprint, it is necessary to access the areas of your biocomputer mind where unconscious habits are stored in the form of mental image pictures. The good news about this is that, in the last few years, increasingly effective techniques have been developed for reaching these habit storage areas and erasing their negative expressions. These methods can work for a variety of other unwanted habits as well as your unwanted astrological ones.

In chapters 3 and 4 you will learn techniques for opening the doors to where your subconscious habits are stored. Once the doors are open, there are many ways to reprogram negative habits. In following chapters we will show you how to apply some of these reprogramming techniques to each zodiac sign and also to other important astrological factors.

As an example of how astrological energies can be reprogrammed, I (Mary) have Saturn in a strong position in my horoscope, which tends to make me rather cautious. However a pattern that includes Mars in Aries tends toward unconsidered, quick-on-the-trigger action. A few years ago I was in a car crash after impulsively turning in front of an oncoming car without looking carefully. I had expressed the cautious pattern by fastening my safety belt and, although the car was totaled, I came out with only a bruise where the seat belt had held me from flying through the windshield.

When I got home, I checked out the pattern of the planets at the time of the accident and saw that Mars had been connecting with my horoscope in a way that has been found to amplify an impulsive pattern. I began using some of the visualization techniques to be described later for programming a healthy balance between the cautious Saturn and the impulsive Mars in Aries, directing myself to be wary where it was needed, but not to let this prevent spontaneous action where that was called for.

Mars has a two-year cycle around the zodiac. Two years later I was again driving when Mars was in the same triggering position, but this time I was aware of it. Another car was driving ahead of mine on a narrow country road where traffic was rare, and a large bulldozer pulled over to let this car pass. My impulse was to continue closely behind the other car, but caution stepped in and I paused. The bulldozer operator, evidently not expecting two cars at once on the sparsely traveled road, failed to check his rearview mirror and immediately moved back across the road after the front car had passed, which would have forced my car into the steep ditch if I had followed my first impulse.

But over and beyond the preventing of an accident, I found that I was now expressing this balance between the Mars and Saturn energies in more self-fulfilling ways. As a writer I had always been troubled by a need to structure what I was saying absolutely right the first time (Saturn), yet my Mars energy wanted to push ahead without having to weigh what I was trying to write. I wrote very slowly, pulling out every word like deeply rooted stumps, and underneath this agonizing process I could feel impatient Mars, like a racehorse hitched to a plow. But after the Mars–Saturn energies became better balanced, the writing began to flow with a spontaneity and freedom that still took into account the structure and train of thought that Saturn wanted.

Your horoscope is like a musical instrument with incredible potential for expressing your beauty and uniqueness. This expression is most fulfilling when you become aware of what your instrument is capable of doing for you and when you appreciate the kind of music that your unique horoscope is designed to play best, its most satisfying modes of expression. In addition, it is necessary to tune it and learn to play it so that its patterns interact harmoniously. And lastly, your effectiveness is increased when you recognize the kind of music that is called for at a given time. As Shakespeare said in *Julius Caesar*, "There is a tide in the affairs of men, which, taken at the flood, leads on to fortune."

How far can we go in reprogramming negative astrological patterns? That question cannot be fully answered, but the evidence is increasing that, as is being found in other areas of the psyche, we have considerably more potential than we might ever have imagined even in our wildest dreams!

When you have applied the techniques in this book, prepare to be astounded! And let us know what happens—we are working on another book, describing the results experienced by people in all sorts of situations.

But before we get to the techniques (beginning in chapter 3), it can be helpful to understand more about the latest scientific research that may explain *why* astrology works. This is the subject of the next chapter.

SUMMARY

1. Astrology is the study of patterns in the heavens (macrocosm) as reflected in events and in patterns of behavior on Earth (microcosm).

2. These patterns, or themes, can be expressed by a variety of specific actions and events.

3. You will learn techniques that can reprogram your subconscious mind so that astrological energies that had been negatively expressed are rechanneled into self-fulfilling powers.

4. *Horoscope* is from the Greek *horo*, hour, and *skopos*, watcher. It has come to mean the map of the sky as it appeared from the birthplace at the birth time of an individual or at any other significant moment.

5. The Sun, Moon, and each planet have been found to symbolize different functions in your life.

6. The zodiac sign each planet was in when you were born seems to modify the expression of the planet.

7. Being able to reach deep power sources can greatly increase your potential for living in a creative, satisfying, and spiritually harmonious manner.

8. Astrological patterns are, in themselves, neither positive nor negative. The problems and potentials of these patterns depend on how we react to them.

9. When the archetypes in our collective unconscious— including those of astrology—are activated in our personal lives, this tremendous power is going to be expressed in one manner or another. But these expressions can take myriad forms, both powerfully destructive and powerfully creative. This book is about rechanneling the energies of astrological archetypes that can greatly enrich your life.

10. Your horoscope is like a musical instrument with incredible potential for expressing your beauty and uniqueness. This expression is most fulfilling when you become aware of what your instrument is capable of doing for you and when you appreciate the kind of music that your unique horoscope is designed to play best, its most satisfying modes of expression. In addition, it is necessary to tune it and learn to play it, so that its patterns interact harmoniously.

NOTES

1. Karen Hamaker-Zondag, *Astro-Psychology* (Wellingborough, Northamptonshire, Great Britain: Aquarian Press, 1980).

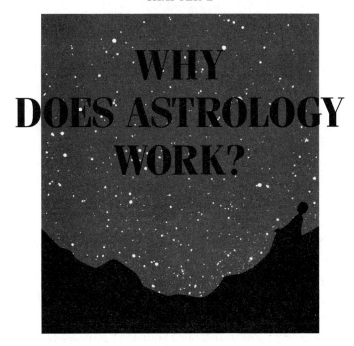

CHAPTER 2

WHY DOES ASTROLOGY WORK?

*A most unfailing experience . . . of the excitement
of sublunary [that is, human] natures by the conjunctions
and aspects of the planets has instructed and
compelled my unwilling belief.*

JOHANN KEPLER, *Larousse Encyclopedia of Astrology*[1]

The universe as a whole is a moving causal network.

DAVID BOHM, *Science, Order, and Creativity*

*At every step along the way, every entity is connected to the
great web of information that is the universe.*

GEORGE LEONARD, The Silent Pulse

*The capability of changing destiny by what
we know as human free will does not necessarily
contradict the mechanistic world view of our universe.
The trick is to reach another dimension and change what
might have been a predictable picture. By achieving an
altered state of consciousness, the predictability of the
mechanistic view of our universe no longer applies.*

PHILIP S. BERG, *The Star Connection*

*The cosmos is a chaotic frenzy of wave patterns,
some of which have been orchestrated on earth into an
organized life system. The harmony between the two can be
understood only with the aid of a score, and of all the
possibilities open to us at this moment, astrology (for all its
weird origins and sometimes weirder devotees) seems to
offer the best interpretation.*

LYALL WATSON, *Super Nature*

✻

It is a crystal clear night and you are standing in the middle of a large dark field, looking up. You pick out familiar features in the heavens—the Big Dipper, Orion, and the path the ancients named the Milky Way because they thought it was like a trail of milk spilled across the sky.

You also trace another sky path, the zodiac. Although this path is not marked by anything as obvious as spilled milk, you have learned to recognize the constellations of stars in front of which the Sun, Moon, and planets move in their eternal rounds.

Your eyes follow the zodiac from eastern to western horizon, looking for travelers on this road, and you are rewarded by seeing, well above the eastern horizon, a bright "star" with a distinctly reddish cast—Mars. You think about the space probe that landed on this neighbor planet, and how the pictures sent back showed the red desert you are now seeing.

Farther along on the zodiac trail you see another bright traveler with a whiter glow. You know that this one is Jupiter, and you picture its herd of moons, invisible to your naked eyes but a wonderful sight through a telescope.

Your consciousness expands out in space until you see Earth, Mars, Jupiter, and the other planets, with their moons, circling the Sun.

Then the whole solar system becomes a point of light, one of the points of light making up an outer trailing stream of our spiraling Milky Way galaxy. You know that our whole galaxy is one being in the supergalactic pattern.

*

But all that seems infinitely remote, and the planets—as beautiful as they are—still look very, very far away. How could they have any connection with you personally or with the events in your life?

It's likely that at least part of your mind doesn't believe there is such a connection. Convincing that doubting part can strengthen the reprogramming process you will be learning in the major portion of this book.

The reason we feel skepticism about a meaningful relationship between the cosmos and ourselves is that the scientific and commonsense ideas we grew up with simply didn't allow for this possibility. It was granted that the Sun and Moon affect the Earth with light and gravitational pulls, but it did not seem reasonable that the relatively minor changes in intensity of these influences could have any importance other than enabling us to see our way around and to plan when to launch our ships on the high tides. And the planets and stars—pinpoints of light with virtually undetectable gravitational influences—how could these possibly affect us?

Of course, everyone who has worked at all deeply with astrology has watched, with a sense of wonder, how the flow of events is mirrored symbolically in the positions of the planets. But the majority of scientists have considered such connections to be coincidences, things that just happened to take place at the same time but were not related by cause and effect—the only relationship between phenomena acceptable in traditional scientific thought. So long as there was no conceptual framework for the kind of cosmos–Earth connections that astrology claims, the tendency was to deny the whole thing. One of the important contributions of science has been to free human beings from erroneous beliefs, and it seemed to many people that denying validity to astrology was just another instance in which science was helping us come out from the dark ages of superstition.

However, in spite of the fact that science had decided astrology didn't make sense, investigators in the twentieth century began to uncover increasing evidence of connections between the solar system and what happens on Earth. As Robert A. Millikan, Nobel Prize winner and former president of the California Institute of Technology, has said, "I do not know all the influences which go from body to body. I do know that if man is not affected in some way by the planets, Sun, and Moon, he is the only thing on Earth that isn't."[2]

There are many examples of these connections. For one, studies by biologists have observed a surprising variety of close connections between the phases of the Moon and living creatures. If you are in Southern California during the summer, you could find out when the next new moon or full moon is coming up and go to the beach to watch the grunion spawn. The grunion is a slender, six-inch-long fish with a bluish-green back, and it doesn't need an almanac to know the dates of the new and full moons as well as when to expect the very highest tides during these peak tide periods every month.

Around half an hour after the night's high tide, the fish begin coming ashore. At the height of their spawning run, they turn the wet beach into a shimmering silver sheet. The eggs are laid and fertilized at the high tide rim of the beach. They incubate for two weeks until the next new or full moon brings a peak tide that reaches their sandy nest and washes the newly hatched small fry out to sea. This exquisite timing is necessary so the eggs won't be washed out of the sand before their two-week incubation period is up.

We don't know how the grunion manages this feat of timing, but it is not alone. Many other animals, plants—and also human beings—mirror the Moon's phases in their own ways.

Also, naturalists have shown that events around the birth time can create particularly strong *imprints*—patterns that the living being continues to express. In Disneyland a human in a Donald Duck costume can sometimes be seen walking around followed by a string of real little ducklings. The reason they stick with Donald is that he was the first moving thing they saw after hatching, and that *imprint* sets the pattern that they follow. If their real mother went quacking off in another direction, they would ignore her and be loyal to Donald.

For many living beings the period around birth has been found to be crucially important for setting future patterns of behavior.

Finally, statisticians have found that the positions of certain planets at the time of an individual's birth are related to characteristics that he or she expresses.

*

Imagine that you look east for twenty-four hours, as the Earth makes a complete revolution. You watch the Sun rise at dawn and reach its highest point at noon. During the course of your watch the Moon rises and, a few hours later, culminates. After dark you see Mars rise, brighter and redder than the surrounding stars. It, too, culminates in its own time.

*

What was rising or culminating at the place and time of your birth?

If it happened to be Mars, you are far more likely than average to become a sports champion. On the other hand, if Saturn was your rising or culminating planet, you are more likely to achieve success in science and medicine.

These conclusions are based on extensive and repeated studies that have produced highly significant statistical results correlating planet positions in the sky at the time of birth with future professional success. In some cases the probability of pure chance was one in five million.[3]

Factual evidence continues to accumulate for a variety of the claims astrologers have made. But this evidence, however strong, cannot explain *why* these mysterious connections work. The many scientists who have objected to astrology have done so because its claims have seemed to contradict some of the laws of nature as we understand them. The only thing that can turn this situation around is a new understanding of the "nature" of nature, one in which the evidence for astrology fits in a meaningful way.

THE NEW SCIENTIFIC FRAMEWORK

Surprisingly, it turns out that this new understanding is exactly what has been growing at the edge of scientific thought. This revolution is creating a framework that begins to explain all sorts of mysterious things, including astrology.

In the bibliography we list some books that will tell you more about these scientific breakthroughs, but for now we will tell you only enough so that you can comprehend the importance of cosmic connections. Then (in chapters 3 and 4), we will get right into techniques for working with these connections.

This major change of atmosphere has been taking place in our Western culture's science since the beginning of the twentieth century, and increasingly in the last few decades. Some of the basic assumptions made by scientists in past centuries have been shaken to their roots. Even more unsettling, it is becoming clear in many ways that how we experience reality is often quite different from what's actually going on.

A clear example, of course, is that the science of the past—and commonsense observation—tells us that everything in the heavens goes around the Earth. But Copernicus, Galileo, Kepler, and some of their contemporaries established that this is only the way things appear from a rotating Earth—the more basic motion is that of the Earth around the Sun.

Likewise, the science of recent centuries—and our commonsense experiences—tells us that we live in an objective three-dimensional space in which time flows steadily from the past, through the present, toward the future. Space and time seem to be an independent framework for what happens. We observe that things that are close together affect each other in the strongest manner and that influences get weaker with distance. We also observe that things that happened in the past cause things that happen in the present, and that what is going to happen in the future can be predicted as the effect of causes in the past or present. Such commonsense observations are in accord with scientific laws that were formulated by past investigators, especially in the seventeenth, eighteenth, and nineteenth centuries. This scientific framework has enabled us to understand and control our environment in ways unprecedented in recorded history.

However, more and more investigators began to observe more and more phenomena that didn't fit into the old scientific structure. Theoreticians like Einstein began to construct a new framework that could explain these observed facts. And in so doing they undermined both the old scientific structure and our commonsense "reality" of space, time, and causality.

Key concepts in the new scientific framework are that matter and energy cannot be separated and that the fields surrounding matter are basic to understanding phenomena within these fields. As mentioned earlier, this includes not only local fields like the force around a magnet or the gravitational pull of the Earth, but also larger fields of the physical universe and new kinds of fields — biological and consciousness fields.

In the old viewpoint, matter created any field around it. In the new viewpoint the field can be primary. There is a feedback loop in which the field structures the matter within it and the qualities of the matter modify the field. This goes on from the field of our universe through the series of subfields — our galaxy, our solar system, the Earth, each being on the Earth, down to the basic subatomic particles of the matter we are made of.

Going even further, it is being understood that fields operate on a different level of reality than that of our ordinary world of three-dimensional space and one-way time, in which causes are always earlier than effects.

Many scientific thinkers are also seeing that, just as matter and *energy* cannot be separated, so also matter and *consciousness* are inseparable.

The implications of these developments are being set forth in astounding ways by a growing number of investigators in physics and biology — sciences that, up until this century, had been both the formulators and the strongest supporters of the old scientific framework.

Consider the following statements by a variety of people, some of whom are acknowledged leaders in the world of science:

> The universe does not exist "out there" independent of us. We are inescapably involved in bringing about that which appears to be happening. We are not only observers. We are participators. In some strange sense this is a *participatory universe.*
>
> PHYSICIST JOHN WHEELER[4]

> Nature is part of us, as we are part of it. We can recognize ourselves in the description we give to it.
>
> ILYA PRIGOGINE, CHEMIST
> AND NOBEL PRIZE WINNER[5]

> Present-day developments in cosmology are coming to suggest rather insistently that everyday

conditions could not persist but for the distant parts of the Universe, that all our ideas of space and geometry would become entirely invalid if the distant parts of the Universe were taken away. Our everyday experience even down to the smallest details seems to be so closely integrated to the grand-scale features of the Universe that it is well-nigh impossible to contemplate the two being separated.

ASTRONOMER FRED HOYLE[6]

The world . . . appears as a complicated tissue of events, in which connections of different kinds alternate or overlap or combine and thereby determine the texture of the whole.

PHYSICIST WERNER HEISENBERG[7]

All there is, is the one-verse, the universe looking at itself in itself . . . put simply, the more you interact with the universe, the more you know.

SCIENCE WRITER BOB TOBEN
AND PHYSICIST FRED ALAN WOLF[8]

THE HOLOGRAPHIC UNIVERSE

One of the physicists on the leading edge of the new science is Dr. David Bohm, who was an associate of Einstein's. After many years of considering these matters, in the 1980s, Bohm began to tie his insights together into a far-reaching conceptual framework. Essentially, he says that the universe has two quite different ways in which it is ordered.

One order is our ordinary world, in which objects are located in space and move in time from the past, through the present, toward the future. This he calls the *explicate* or *unfolded* order. The other order is the *implicate*, or *enfolded*, order—that which underlies the explicate manifestations (or unfoldings) of our perceived reality.

In order to make it easier to grasp this concept, Bohm pictures the universe as a stupendous multidimensional hologram. The hologram is a rather spectacular invention made in the 1960s. Its principle was discovered in 1947 but a model could not actually be built until the invention of the laser.

When you look at a hologram you see, suspended in space, a three-dimensional image that you can view from various angles.

Holograms are a form of photography, but photography that works on completely different principles from those of the photography produced by the ordinary cameras with which we are familiar.

✳

To understand the hologram you can imagine: A pool of water whose surface is perfectly still. You drop a pebble in the pool and watch the ripples spread out in concentric circles. Then you drop two pebbles at the same time in different parts of the pool and watch how their circles of ripples meet each other and interact.

Next you drop three pebbles in different places, one after the other. Now you see that the pattern of ripples becomes even more complex. When the first pebble's circle of ripples has spread about two feet away from its center, the second pebble's ripples are less than a foot in diameter, and the third pebble's circle is even smaller. How these ripple patterns intermesh with each other is related to both where and when the pebbles were dropped into the water. If you instantly froze the surface of the pool, you would get a picture of the complex interference pattern from the ripples.

✳

Holography works like this except that it uses light instead of pebbles. As Lyall Watson puts it:

> Light waves behave in exactly the same way. The purest kind of light available to us is that produced by a laser, which sends out a beam in which all the waves are of one frequency, like those made by an ideal pebble in a perfect pond. When two laser beams touch, they produce an interference pattern of light and dark ripples that can be recorded on a photographic plate. And if one of the beams, instead of coming directly from the laser, is reflected first off an object such as a human face, the resulting pattern will be very complex indeed, but it can still be recorded.[9]

If you look at the photographic plate made for a hologram, you will see a frozen instant in the interference pattern of ripples from light waves reflected off the face — an infinitely more complex version of the ripples from the pebbles in the pond. Just as the pattern on the pond's surface looks nothing like the three pebbles, the interference pattern on the photographic plate looks nothing like a face or even anything remotely resembling it. But—and here things become exciting—if you shine laser beams back through the developed photographic film, you will project a three-dimensional image of the face into space.

Now let us cut the photographic film in half. We know what would happen if we did that with an ordinary photograph: one half of the film would show part of the face and the other half would show the rest of it. But that's not what happens with the holographic film—*if you shine lasers through either half, you will get a hologram of the entire face.*

To carry things even further, if you cut the film up into small pieces, any one of them could be used to project an image of the whole face—a fuzzier version, but nevertheless the whole face. In other words, in a hologram *every part of the image interpenetrates every other part, in the same way that Bohm's implicate order universe interpenetrates all its explicate order parts.*

THE HOLOGRAPHIC BRAIN

Besides being a model for how the universe is reflected in its parts, the holographic principle has been seen as an explanation for how the brain processes information. Brain scientists have been increasingly puzzled by investigations that showed, contrary to what had previously been assumed, that memories are not localized in particular cells or regions of the brain but are distributed throughout it. Dr. Karl Pribram, neurophysiologist and Nobel Prize winner, suggests that, as in a hologram, the sensations coming into the brain distribute themselves over large regions of the brain and, when recalled, become specific memories. Thus, there is reason to think that *our brains construct "hard" reality by interpreting frequencies from a dimension transcending time and space. The brain is a hologram, interpreting a holographic universe.*

George Leonard has expressed this concept beautifully:

> At every step along the way, every entity is connected to the great web of information that is the universe. . . . As part of the web, each of us *is* an individual identity, and that identity can be most easily expressed as a wave function, a unique rhythmic pulse. Simultaneously, paradoxically,

each of us *is* a holoid [hologram] of the universe, and that holoid is also expressed in terms of wave functions. Thus, we are both individual and universal, and the web of relationship involves both aspects of our being.[10]

THE FIELDS OF LIFE

This new understanding of the background fields and how they connect with manifested reality is beginning to solve long-standing puzzles in biology that the old scientific framework could not explain.

Traditional biology looks to the genes to explain why a fertilized rabbit egg grows into a rabbit rather than a cat. Researchers are beginning to comprehend how genes code information for the sequence of chemical building blocks in RNA and protein molecules. But this understanding of the fine structure of living matter falls far short of accounting for the complex structures developed by living beings or for their complex patterns of behavior.

The idea of fields in biology is not a new one. Through the years many investigators have felt that some kind of field could account for what isn't explained in the fine structure — the genes — of living beings. This search in biology is rather similar to what had been going on at the same time in physics. Advances in the understanding of how fields worked explained phenomena that could not be accounted for by the fine structure of matter — the subatomic particles.

A principal leading edge thinker in biology is Dr. Rupert Sheldrake, a biochemist from Cambridge University. He has focused on the mystery of how things take their shape, or *morphogenesis*. In pointing out why the action of the genes cannot account for complex forms and patterns of behavior in living beings, he has said: "It is as if the delivery of the right building materials and machinery to plots of ground resulted in the spontaneous growth of houses of just the right form."[11]

To put together the building blocks, Sheldrake's hypothesis of *formative causation* proposes a special kind of formative field — the *morphic field* (shortened from *morphogenetic*), or *M-field*. He says that:

> Each kind of natural system has its own kind of field: there is an insulin field, a beech field, a swallow field, and so on. Such fields shape all the

25

different kinds of atoms, molecules, crystals, living organisms, societies, customs, and habits of mind.[12]

Sheldrake has used the analogy of a television set: The pictures on the screen arise in the television studio and are transmitted through the electromagnetic field as vibrations of a particular frequency. These would correspond to the morphic field. But to produce the pictures on the screen, the set must contain the right components wired up in the right way. These components correspond to the genes. Changes in the components, such as a fault in a transistor, can alter or even abolish the pictures on the screen.

Sheldrake carries the concept of morphic fields even further, suggesting that we could "regard entire planets as organisms with characteristic morphic fields, and likewise planetary systems, stars, galaxies, and clusters of galaxies. . . . Perhaps it makes sense to think of the entire universe as an all-inclusive organism [with] a morphic field which would include, influence, and interconnect the morphic fields of all the organisms it contains."[13]

In describing the dynamics of the morphic fields and the organisms within them he sees a "two-way flow of influence: from fields to organisms and from organisms to fields. . . . All organisms are dynamic structures that are continuously recreating themselves under the influence of their own past states."[14]

In other words, both the forms that organisms develop and the patterns of behavior that they manifest are directed by characteristic morphic fields: those that are specific to particular kinds of organisms, those that include all organisms, the field of our planet, that of our solar system, right up to the universal field. And as the habits built into these fields influence the organisms within them, so also the individual actions of the organisms modify the fields.

Sheldrake believes that if his morphic, or *M-field*, hypothesis is proven correct, it may go a long way toward explaining psychologist Carl Jung's notion of a *collective unconscious* as well as leading to very different interpretations of phenomena in parapsychology.

Jung's idea of the collective unconscious was formulated as a result of his years of observation that the same basic themes were expressed by individuals and cultures all over the world. As mentioned earlier, he called these *archetypes* and he was well aware of the power with which they can move us. In the light of Sheldrake's concept, the archetypes could be considered fields into which we connect through morphic resonance. And, as we have already pointed out, the signs of the zodiac, planets, and other factors in astrology can be considered archetypes.

THE CHARACTER OF THE MOMENT

In the course of his work, Jung became increasingly aware of the qualities of a particular time. He observed that "we are born at a given moment, in a given place, and we have, like the best wines, the quality of the year and the season which witness our birth." Jung used horoscopes of his patients to help understand them. He also saw that certain apparently unrelated events that seem just to happen at the same time—coincidences—have a relationship that doesn't fit into normal cause-and-effect connections. He called this relationship *synchronicity* and described it as an "acausal connecting principle."

In the old scientific framework, such a connection was nonsense, but in the new framework, the door has been opened to understanding how synchronicity arises "out of the underlying patterns of the universe rather than through a causality of pushes and pulls that we normally associate with events in nature."[15]

SCIENCE AND SPIRIT

Thus, some of the recent concepts in physics, biology, and psychology have begun to sound like worldwide spiritual inspirations that see all manifestation as connected to a larger reality—a reality in which consciousness and matter are inexorably intertwined.

> To See a World in a Grain of Sand,
> And Heaven in a Wild Flower,
> Hold Infinity in the palm of your hand,
> And Eternity in an hour.
>
> WILLIAM BLAKE, *Auguries of Innocence*

> The body of man is related to our entire galaxy and universe.
>
> ZOHAR I

> In the heaven of Indra there is said to be a network of pearls so arranged that if you look at one you see all the others reflected in it. In the same way, each object in the world is not merely itself but

involves every other object, and in fact *is* every
other object.

SIR CHARLES ELIOT, Japanese Buddhism[16]

The heavens declare the glory of God; and the
firmament showeth his handiwork.
Day unto day uttereth speech, and night unto
night showeth knowledge.
There is no speech nor language where their voice
is not heard.
Their line is gone out through all the earth, and
their words to the end of the world. In them
hath he set a tabernacle for the sun,
Which is as a bridegroom coming out of his cham-
ber, and rejoiceth as a strong man to run his
course.
His going forth is from the end of the heavens, and
his circuit unto the ends of it; and there is nothing hid from the heat thereof.

PSALM 19:1–6, KJV

THE UNIVERSAL HOLOGRAM

From many directions we have come to the realization that each
individual is intimately related to the universe. Each of us can be
considered a piece of the universal hologram, and thus we carry the
pattern of the whole, not only in our birth imprint but also in the
ongoing "holomovement."

We can also visualize the universe as a cosmic orchestra in
which each of us is a particular instrument in the Earth's part of
our solar system section.

We respond to a complex network of fields; at the "matter pole"
they include gravitational, electromagnetic, quantum, and also the
morphic fields of our biological forms. At the "consciousness pole"
we respond to the archetypes of our collective unconscious, our
cultural patterns, and our individual patterns of awareness and
action. These archetypes can be seen as universal principles in
their purest form, and some of the archetypes are associated with
planets, signs of the zodiac, and other components of the cosmic
field.

As we resonate with the archetypes, we manifest particular
expressions of them, habits in their fields. And not only are we

28

influenced by habits in an archetypal field, but as we express the archetypes, we also contribute to the modification of these habits — it's a two-way process. We can change discordant habits in the archetypes.

MAKING CHANGES

How do we go about altering such habit patterns? That they do change is obvious when we look at both cultures and individuals. We can be locked into the phases of an old pattern and then something shifts, and the old pattern is noticeably modified or a new one emerges. As Prigogine has put it:

> We know that we can interact with nature.... Matter is not inert. It is alive and active. Life is always changing one way or another through its adaptation to nonequilibrium conditions. *With the idea of a doomed determinist world view now gone, we can feel free to make our fate for good or ill.* [emphasis ours][17]

One way to look at changing our destiny is by considering an idea that takes our minds another step into a new frame — the concept of parallel universes. Physicist Hugh Everett III came to the conclusion that we live in an infinite number of continually interacting universes. Moreover, in this system of an infinite number of parallel universes "all possible futures really happen."[18]

Other physicists are also entertaining this concept. Science writer Michael Talbot describes a conversation he had with Alan Guth, a physicist from M.I.T.:

> He confessed that if pressed for an answer, he favored the Many Worlds Hypothesis. When I asked him if this meant that there were, at that moment, a multitude of Alan Guths and Michael Talbots carrying on similar conversations in an indefinite number of parallel universes, with obvious reluctance he replied, "Yes. We can't communicate with each other, but we all exist. It's mind-boggling. But it is actually the simplest interpretation of quantum mechanics, or at least I think so."[19]

We could visualize our consciousness shifting from one parallel universe to another, from one dance with the cosmic music into a different dance, thus *changing our destiny.*

✳

We have recounted some of the recent breakthroughs in understanding *why* we, as individuals, are connected to universal patterns. Now it is time to look at some recent breakthroughs in understanding *how* we can change the ways in which these patterns manifest themselves.

In all ages and cultures people have connected with the energies of various archetypal patterns by refocusing consciousness, tuning in through music, dance, ritual, prayer, meditation, and in many other ways. And in recent years great strides have been made in developing highly effective ways to use natural skills that refocus consciousness, skills involving relaxation and visualization, not only to connect with inner patterns but also to harmonize discordant ones and heal body, mind, and life expressions.

The next two chapters will tell you about some of these rather amazing developments and then get down to specific techniques that have helped many people change unwanted patterns, be healed, and actualize potentials they had only dreamed of. We will, of course, put special emphasis on techniques that can be applied to changing unwanted astrological habits.

Then, beginning with chapter 5, "The Transforming Zodiac," we will be dealing specifically with the astrological patterns you may wish to change.

SUMMARY

1. Factual evidence continues to accumulate for a variety of the claims astrologers have made.

2. Developments at the leading edge of scientific understanding are creating a theoretical framework that begins to explain astrology.

3. Key concepts in the new scientific framework are that matter and energy cannot be separated and that the fields surrounding matter are basic to understanding phenomena within these fields, including the larger fields of the physical universe and new kinds of fields—biological and consciousness fields.

4. It is thought that the universe works like a hologram, in which every part interpenetrates every other part. Any change is transmitted to the whole.

5. It is also thought that our brains construct "reality" by interpreting frequencies from a dimension transcending time and space. Thus, the brain is a hologram, interpreting a holographic universe. Each of us can be considered a piece of the universal hologram, and thus we carry the pattern of the whole, not only in our birth imprint but also in the ongoing "holomovement."

6. A special kind of formative field, or morphic field, has been proposed for each kind of natural system, atoms, living organisms, customs, habits of mind, planetary systems, galaxies.

7. Archetypes, including the signs of the zodiac, planets, and other factors in astrology, can be considered fields into which we connect through morphic resonance.

8. There is a feedback loop in which the field structures the matter within it and the qualities of the matter modify the field. All organisms are dynamic structures that are continuously re-creating themselves under the influence of their own past states.

9. As we resonate with the archetypes, we manifest particular expressions of them, "habits" in their fields. Not only are we influenced by habits in an archetypal field, we also contribute to the modification of these habits as we express the archetypes.

10. We could look at changing our destiny as accessing a parallel universe, from one dance with the cosmic music to a different dance.

11. In all ages and cultures people have connected with archetypal patterns by refocusing consciousness, tuning in through music, dance, ritual, prayer, meditation, and in many other ways.

12. In recent years, highly effective ways of using natural skills to refocus consciousness have been developed.

NOTES

1. Quoted by Jean-Louis Brau, Helen Weaver, and Allan Edmands in *Larousse Encyclopedia of Astrology* (New York: McGraw-Hill, 1977), 164–65.
2. Quoted by Paul Katzeff in *Full Moons* (Secaucus, N.J.: Citadel Press, 1981).
3. Dr. Michel Gauquelin is a Sorbonne-trained psychologist and statistician who is director of the Laboratory for the Study of the Relationship Between Cosmic and Psycho-Physiological Rhythms in Paris, France. Since 1949 Gauquelin has collected the birth data of many thousands of people and studied the correlation of personality traits and later choice of profession with the positions of certain planets at the birth time, as oriented to the birth place. These studies were checked against control groups and some of them have been replicated by other investigators. Gauquelin has continued to confirm his results by analyzing birth data on thousands more people.

However, the implications of this work appear inevitably to support certain astrological tenets that have seemed totally impossible to reconcile with the prevailing scientific view of how things connect. Therefore, Gauquelin's work drew harsh criticism from quite a few individuals in the scientific field.

The controversy around Gauquelin has been long and bitter, but the bottom line is that trained, impartial observers confirm both the soundness of his methodology and his conclusions. Critics who called his work fraudulent or inconclusive have denied crucial basic data or, in some cases, seem to have actually fudged their own data. Generally these criticisms have been published in scientific journals and the countering evidence of Gauquelin and his supporters has been denied. For an accurate, detailed, and funny history of this controversy see the forthcoming edition of *The Case for Astrology* by John Anthony West and Jan Toonder (Penguin-Viking, 1990).

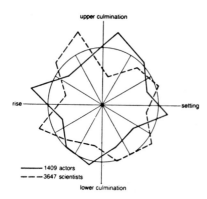

upper culmination

rise — setting

——— 1409 actors
— — — 3647 scientists

lower culmination

Figure 1. Jupiter positions in the natal horoscopes of actors and scientists. (Copyright © 1981 by Michel Gauquelin from the book *Your Personality and the Planets.* Reprinted with permission of Stein and Day publishers.)

The position of Jupiter at the birth of actors is very different from its position at the birth of scientists. The times favoring the birth of successful actors (black line) correspond to the times that prevent the birth of successful scientists (dotted line). The circle indicates the frequency of ordinary births. This antagonistic pattern is statistically remarkable.

4. Quoted by Larry Dossey, M.D., in *The American Theosophist* (Fall Special Issue, 1982), 324.
5. Ibid., 312
6. Fred Hoyle, *Frontiers of Astronomy* (New York: Harper, 1955), 304.
7. Werner Heisenberg, *Physics and Philosophy* (New York: Harper Torchbooks, 1958), 158.

8. Toben and Wolf, *Space-Time and Beyond* (New York: E. P. Dutton, 1975), 128.
9. Quoted by Marilyn Ferguson, *The Aquarian Conspiracy* (Los Angeles: J. P. Tarcher, 1980), 178.
10. George Leonard, *The Silent Pulse* (New York: Bantam, 1981), 78.
11. Rupert Sheldrake, *The Presence of the Past: Morphic Resonance and the Habits of Nature* (New York: Times Books, 1988), 91.
12. Ibid., xviii.
13. Ibid., 300–1.
14. Ibid., 133.
15. F. David Peat, *Synchronicity* (New York: Bantam, 1987), 16.
16. Sir Charles Eliot, *Japanese Buddhism* (New York: Barnes & Noble, 1969), 109–10, writing about the *Avalamsaka Sutra.*
17. Quoted by M. Lukas, "The World According to Ilya Prigogine," *Quest/80* (Dec. 1980), 88.
18. Toben and Wolf, *Space-Time and Beyond*, 13.
19. Michael Talbot, *Beyond the Quantum: God, Reality, Consciousness in the New Scientific Revolution* (New York: Macmillan, 1987), 151.

CHAPTER 3

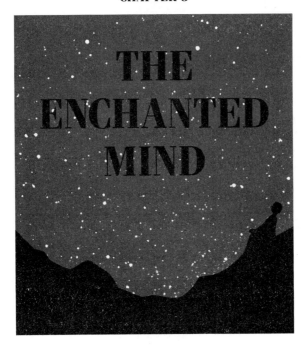

Whatever is believed becomes reality
and all possible pasts, presents, and futures are like
different channels on a television set.
MICHAEL TALBOT, *Mysticism and the New Physics*

Once upon a time in ancient China there was an emperor named
Kru Won, a clever but cruel ruler who governed with an iron will.
He had many wives who were guarded by the royal eunuchs while
he entertained himself with gambling and his subjects with public
games. Unfortunately, one of the emperor's most trusted generals
fell in love with one of Kru Won's favorite wives and ran away with
her. They were captured and returned to the court of Kru Won for
punishment.

Rather than having their heads cut off, as was the usual custom,
the emperor decided that a little entertainment for the court might
be amusing. He had the general placed in the middle of an amphi-
theater that had two doors. Leaning from the balcony toward the

general he said, "You must choose to open one of the two doors. Behind one I have placed a beautiful unmarried maiden, behind the other a tiger which we have starved for a week.

"So, my friend, you will be either married or eaten alive. My wife who sits next to me, who has also shared your bed, knows where I have placed the maiden and the tiger. Since you two have vowed undying love for one another, I have given her permission to tell you what is behind the doors."

The general looked up at his lover and she pointed to the door on the left. He immediately went over to the door and opened it.

✳

Did he find the beautiful maiden or the ravenous tiger?

The answer you just thought of is very important to you. It will give you an idea about how you move through life—with trust or distrust, optimism or pessimism. We will be discussing this later in the chapter and will give you the answer to the riddle.

THE POWER OF ATTENTION AND THE HOLOGRAPHIC MIND

The mind has been likened to a biocomputer. The very quality of our lives depends on whether we are its masters or slaves. Your understanding of this tool is the key to shaping your future and that of the world, for it is an amazing tool of unlimited potential.

In all ages certain people have realized some of this potential. However, in recent times our Western culture has downplayed or denied the role of mind over matter. In this section of the book we describe how awareness of the mind's vast powers has been reappearing in many fields of knowledge—not only *what* the mind is capable of, but also *how* to make it happen.

Then, when you have comprehended both what is possible and how to do it, we will return to astrology and focus on reprogramming your conscious and unconscious mindsets.

Your mind is like a camera that takes pictures of events around you. These are very special types of mental images. They store information, retrievable consciously and unconsciously, which consists of what you saw, heard, felt, smelled, and tasted at the time you took the picture. These are what we call our memories or thoughts. The information contained in these mental images is activated by ATTENTION. Attention is the key; it is your power, your rudder, the control stick, the channel changer of your internal television set.

One of today's most amazing scientific theories is that these mental images are like holograms. As explained in chapter 2, holograms are not two-dimensional pictures like the one on the cover of this book, or photos in magazines, or paintings. Holograms are three-dimensional pictures made with laser light. They have become a common item in our everyday life, appearing on charge cards as a three-dimensional icon and sold in gift stores and novelty shops.

As we mentioned in chapter 2, the two main characteristics of holograms are: First, that although if you take a negative of a two-dimensional photograph, cut it up, and project light through one of the pieces, you will get only the part of the image contained in the piece you chose, with a holographic plate the difference is that if you smash it into a thousand pieces and then take one piece and put it in front of a laser light, you get the whole picture. Every part of a hologram contains the image information of the whole. And second, by shifting the angle of the plate, a hologram can receive the information of thousands of pictures on the same plate. By changing the angle of the plate, the picture appears, disappears, and reappears.

These two main characteristics of holograms are what led Pribram to propose the holographic brain theory, as mentioned earlier, to explain some of the previously unexplainable mysteries of how the brain/mind works.

A movie camera takes twenty-four pictures per second in order to simulate the motion of real life on the screen of televisions and cinemas. The mind takes pictures in much the same way. The information in these pictures is then sorted (by deletions, distortions, and generalizations), stored in the brain, and activated by our attention or outside stimulus, which "triggers" the memory.

You can test this information, storage, and retrieval system of our marvelous, magical mind right now. Have your biocomputer put up a picture of a ball on the screen of the internal television set or, as they say, in front of your mind's eye.

Good. There were thousands of pictures of balls you could have selected: footballs, baseballs, soccer balls. Now put that aside and get a picture of a tree, any tree from any time in your life.

Okay, now get a picture of your bedroom. Of your high school building. Of your favorite high school teacher. How about one of a teacher you didn't like? Now think of your grammar school. Can you see the front of the building? How about retrieving a picture of one of your grammar school teachers? Now get a picture of your bedroom at that time.

So now you get the idea. Your mind is a collection of holographic pictures of your past that can be retrieved. It is filled with archaic information. It isn't happening now, though you can have an instant replay of the movie of the incident or memory you are retrieving. It is quite like your family photo album at home. The mind is an archival library. The pictures of the past have nothing to do with the current moment. However, they can impinge on the consciousness of the moment and change your feelings (and even the cells of your body) radically and almost instantly.

We are now going to ask you to remember two events of your life. And then we are going to have you go back to them. But first we just want you to remember the event you pick. Close your eyes if you find it easier to visualize that way, and pick out a memory of a time in your life in which you were very sad or depressed. As soon as you have chosen one, put it aside and get a picture of a time in your life when you were very happy or felt exceptionally powerful.

Now go back to the first picture of the sad or depressing event, sit back, and run the movie of the incident in front of your mind's eye on what we are calling your internal television set. See what you saw then; hear the sounds that were going on then, the voices, perhaps music; feel what you were feeling then; smell the smells, perhaps something cooking or other predominant odors, until you are beginning to actually feel sad or depressed now.

After you have done this, open your eyes and move your body around before you do the next step.

Now get the second picture of a happy or powerful time, close your eyes if it makes it easier, and run the movie — seeing, hearing, feeling, and smelling the sensations of that time until you feel happy and/or powerful, and then open your eyes.

You probably noticed that within a half-minute or less (sometimes it can take only seconds) you began to feel happy or depressed depending on what memories, pictures, or movie you were running. Whichever one you were paying attention to, the one on which you focused your "lens," is the one that influenced your current feelings.

Isn't this an amazing phenomenon? Even if we are having a wonderful day and feeling good, if a depressing memory, for example, "comes into our head" it can make us feel awful, even though that particular thing is not happening *now* and we were previously in a good mood. You have experienced it many times in your day-to-day living.

Let's go a little further in our exploration. Recent experiments at many universities have proven that not only can these holographic pictures influence or change our moods and feelings, but a picture we hold in front of our mind's eye can also influence our body, right down to the cellular level, and in an amazingly short period of time.

In *Omni* (Vol. 5, No. 5, Feb. '83), Marc McCutcheon reported on the results of research done at Pennsylvania State University. Penn State psychologist Howard Hall wanted to test the claim of some doctors that creative imagery helps in combating cancer. He took the white blood cell count of a number of cancer patients and then taught them self-hypnosis, which is basically relaxing the major muscle groups of the body. Once the body is relaxed, the mind follows.

Dr. Hall taught these patients progressive relaxation techniques similar to the ones we will be describing in the next chapter. Then he asked the patients to imagine their white blood cells as powerful and hungry sharks eating up their cancer cells. Children could imagine Pac Man eating up the bad cells. An hour later the white blood count was taken again. Hall instructed his subjects to practice the visualization exercise twice a day for a week and then the white blood count was taken once more.

The results were startling, especially considering that the white blood cells are the body's first line of defense against mutant cancer cells and other foreign invaders of the body. The white blood cell count went, on the average, from 13,508 to 15,192, and a week later was up to 18,950. Some did better than others, but the proof was there. "For some inexplicable reason," said Hall, "the mind can influence the body by changing the bio-chemistry of the blood."[1]

There are many more examples of experiments like this; in fact, they have created a whole new field called psychoimmunology, studying the effect of the controlled use of imagery on the cells and the immune systems of the human body. Many of us grew up with the idea of "mind over matter," but at that time it was just a theory, a philosophy of approaching life. Now it is a scientific fact — whatever image from your mind you pay attention to, especially while relaxed or highly focused, changes not only your feelings and emotions, but also the very cells of your body, and that in a very short time. Even the silly images of a powerful shark or Pac Man eating up bad cells brought about profound physiological changes to the immune system.

POWER OF THE SELF-IMAGE

Your self-image, the picture of who you think you are that you carry, consciously or subconsciously, around with you twenty-four hours a day has a powerful influence on your weight, your health, your prosperity, your self-esteem, your emotions, your spiritual life, your relationships, the very heart and pulse of your life.

Continuing in the exploration of the nature of your mind, we'd like you to make a collage picture of a negative you. That means putting together a composite of every negative thing anyone has ever said about you. You're too tall, too short, too lazy, a liar, fat, too skinny, whatever. Got it?

Now put the first picture aside. The second picture we'd like you to create is an entirely positive picture of yourself. Include every nice thing anyone has ever said about you or you have thought about yourself.

Once you've done that, split the screen of your internal television set, put the two images side by side, and look at them. Interesting? Which one is correct? Which picture can we consider to be a true self-image? Which makes you feel good when you look at it; which doesn't?

Well, neither of the holograms is true or not true. What makes one or the other real or not depends on which one you pay attention to and consider to be true. None of the information in our biocomputers is true per se without our consent and our acting upon the information contained within the hologram. This is the second principle of controlling our minds and becoming the captain of our own ship.

THE SPIRIT, THE MIND, AND THE BODY

For mastery of the personal biocomputer and the shaping of your own future, it is essential to understand not only the holographic nature of the mind and of your thoughts, but also *who you are* in relation to them. You are a *spirit*, infinite and wondrous beyond description. Further definitions of your spiritual nature and origin we will leave up to you and your personal and/or religious upbringing.

We are spirits inhabiting vehicles called human bodies. There aren't too many people in the world who pay attention to spirits *without* bodies, so if one wants to get into *a play on the stage of life,* one must find a pregnant woman and enter the fetus. You've got to buy a ticket to get into the movie. The ticket into the life game as we know it here on Earth is a body. The instrument for controlling the body and moving it about is the mind, through the use of mental images.

We are using the old Greek philosophical trinity of spirit, mind, and body. The mind is the "switchboard" between the spirit and the body. If you want to stand up, you first intend the action and then picture yourself in action, and then (this is greatly simplified) the body executes the thought/picture/holographic program. Of course many of the body's functions are on automatic, like the beating of the heart or breathing, and even these functions can be consciously controlled by the use of imagery and creative visualizations.

YOU ARE NOT YOUR MIND

This way of understanding consciousness is used in Western philosophy almost exclusively to mean a reflexive sort of consciousness, self consciousness, or the distinction between self and other. This distinction is called "intentionality" in philosophy and is based on the idea that *we can tell our own awareness from that which we are aware of.* (italics ours)

KARL PRIBRAM,
The Holographic Hypothesis of Brain Function

What we are looking for is what is looking.

ST. FRANCIS OF ASSISI, quoted by
Marilyn Ferguson in *The Aquarian Conspiracy*

For a moment, let's go back to the statement we made that may have surprised or confused you—that you are not your mind or your thought pictures. When you understand this, you will be able, in a few moments, to give yourself the great gift of personal freedom and peace of mind.

Close this book and hold it in your hand. Make a mental image of it simply by paying attention to it. A holographic reproduction will automatically be made by your mind. Put the book aside, close your eyes, and retrieve the mental hologram you just made. Who are *you* in relation to the picture of the book you just made?

Get a picture of a house out of your mental files. Look at it. Who are *you* in relation to the picture you are observing?

That's right, you are the *looker*, the *observer*, the *witness*, the *viewer* of the picture in front of your mind's eye. If you *were* the thought picture, you wouldn't be able to see it, you would *be* it! Much the same way you can't see your eyes unless you are in front of a mirror.

So you are not any of the memories or thoughts or holograms you've recorded all your life, stored, and been able to retrieve. You, the spirit, decide whether or not to pay attention to the holographic thought pictures in your mental files. *You* have the choice. *You* call the picture up in order to "see" it on the internal television. Even at moments in your life when holographic memories "pop up" on your internal screen (seemingly uninvited)—perhaps restimulated by something in your enviroment, and you just catch yourself watching or "wallowing" in it—you still have the choice to switch channels and simply pay attention to some other hologram memory, or be in present time attending to what you were engaged in the moment before the intrusion.

ATTENTION: WHAT IT IS, WHAT IT DOES

Attention is the process of consciousness
which gives rise to self-reflection.

KARL PRIBRAM

To a great degree, perception *is* reality! What you hear, see, and feel is the reality you experience, because that is the way your neurology is constructed. Your attention is your life force directed or

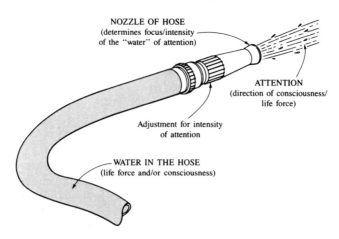

Figure 2. Directing attention.

focused on something outside yourself or on your internal screen. It is like a flashlight in a completely dark room. Whatever you shine your light on is what you are aware of, where you perceive you are. What we call the Law of Attention is this: Whatever you focus your attention on, increases.

Think about the hose in the illustration on page 42. The water in the hose is your consciousness and life force. Wherever you point the hose, the lifegiving waters of your essence and consciousness follow, nurturing and making more real whatever has captured your attention. The diameter of the nozzle is your *focus* and controls the intensity and volume of life force consciousness being directed by your attention.

Attention is one of the aspects of your life that is within your control. If you had a glass of water (see Figure 3 below) would you say it was half empty or half full?

Simplistic? Yes!

Deceptively profound? Yes!

Whatever aspect, viewpoint, attitude you use to approach a situation in your life affects the situation. This is the basis of all stress management techniques.

Look at the line drawn in an arc. Is it concave or convex? Con-

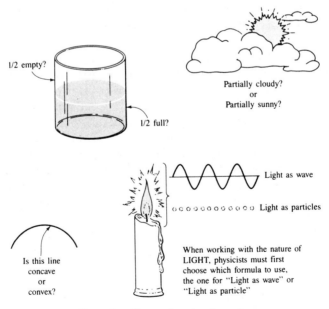

1/2 empty?

1/2 full?

Partially cloudy?
or
Partially sunny?

Is this line
concave
or
convex?

Light as wave

Light as particles

When working with the nature of LIGHT, physicists must first choose which formula to use, the one for "Light as wave" or "Light as particle"

Figure 3. Alternatives in viewpoint.

tinuing with the same theme, given a day with some sunshine, some clouds, would you label the weather partially cloudy or partially clear? As basic as these examples may seem, this technology of attention is in keeping with the latest scientific research on coping with stress and maintaining good physical and mental health, for what matters is not what happens to us in life but what we *do* with what happens to us.

REFRAMING:
TURNING LEMONS INTO LEMONADE

> Sorcerers say that we are inside a bubble. It is a bubble into which we are placed at the moment of our birth. At first the bubble is open, but then it begins to close until it has sealed us in. That bubble is our perception. We live inside that bubble all of our lives. And what we witness on its round walls is our own reflection.
>
> CARLOS CASTANEDA, *Tales of Power*

There is homespun advice that has become a cliché—when life hands you a lemon, make lemonade. In Neuro-Linguistic Programming (N.L.P.) that's called reframing. A *frame* is the way we perceive the world. It is the personal map we use to travel through life. Except that, as Gregory Bateson points out in *Ecology of Mind, the map is not the territory.* For a human to assume that the map is the territory would be as silly as going into a restaurant and eating the menu! The menu is only a linguistic description of the food, not the food itself. We all have pet beliefs, ideas, and models of the way we think the world works or should work. It is our favorite way of viewing reality, though every personal and scientific breakthrough on this planet has come through reframing, or changing the way we see the world. William James, in *Varieties of Religious Experience,* says, "An idea (belief) can galvanize the believer's entire being even though it has no existence. It colors our entire experience of material reality."

If you live in the Western Hemisphere and are walking down a road at night, and all of a sudden hear hoofbeats behind you, how come you don't think it is a zebra?

In the days of Columbus, the accepted map of the world was that it was flat. In the days of Copernicus, the accepted map of the universe put the world at the center of the universe.

Columbus, even after proving that the world was round, was doubted, and it took two generations before the general public's frame of the world changed. Copernicus was forced to withdraw his findings because they went against the accepted model of the world, the current popular belief system. Everyone knows the Sun revolves around the Earth. Just take a look and see, right?

Human beings stubbornly hold on to their beliefs, or frames, or paradigms because, in the case of the flat earth theory, they knew that the world was flat because it appeared so. Perception is considered to be reality by many, despite evidence to the contrary.

How many kinds of snow are there? Two, three? Slush, wet snow, powder snow. . . . Eskimos have words that distinguish over fifty different types of snow. Michael Talbot, in *Mysticism and the New Physics*, quotes Joseph Chilton Pearce as saying that "our reality is 'word-built' simply because our consciousness *creates* our reality, and consciousness, as we have been taught to know it, is primarily experienced linguistically." Eskimos see red snow, blue snow, and so on.

The book you are holding in your hands is not solid. It appears so, but our scientists say it is a mass of rapidly moving molecules with great space in between them all, at least as great (relatively) as the distance between the Earth and the Moon. Now does that seem real to you? But the idea has been proven, and we have accepted the idea of tiny atoms moving rapidly and forming matter that looks solid. As Talbot points out, from Castaneda's books, "Things are real only after one has learned to agree on their realness."

So how you react to something and describe something to yourself or others becomes true for you. If you say you can, you can. Your subconscious will oblige you. If you say you can't, guess what? You can't.

The medical community laughed at William Harvey when he proposed that blood flowed through veins; it thought that washing of hands between operations was superstitious; it told Roger Bannister the human heart wouldn't survive running the mile in under four minutes.

The Wright brothers were laughed at for trying to build a flying machine heavier than air. After all, they were only bicycle repairmen. People laughed at Ford's horseless carriage, or thought it was the work of the devil, black magic.

You can do anything you can dream you can do, no matter what anyone says to the contrary. *You* are in charge of your destiny. The only limitations are the ones you impose on yourself. The only limitations are your belief systems, your personal map of the world—your favorite frame, perspective, or ideas about who you think you are and how the world will respond to you. As Dr. Irving Oyle, whose story about the tiger and the maiden we took the liberty of transforming, said in his wonderful book, *Time, Space and the Mind*, "Are you a pessimist or an optimist? That is, do you believe that the universe which you inhabit is indifferent to your existence and well being? Or, do you believe that the cosmos, our galaxy and our solar system are specifically designed to further your own personal growth, happiness, and evolution?"

A general is losing a battle and reframes the event to his troops by saying, "We're not retreating, we're just advancing in another direction."

A client told us a story about his big nose. He hated it. It was huge. One day his one-year-old daughter wriggled out of his arms too enthusiastically and was falling. She reached up and grabbed his nose. He loves to tell that story.

People made fun of Rudolph's nose until Santa used it to light his way on Christmas night.

This gift of reframing comes naturally to some people. A famous anchorwoman on a major television network was interviewed about her success. She told the story of her first interview at a small midwestern station. She failed miserably. Her mother had driven her to the interview and waited outside. On the way home, in the midst of tears, the future successful anchorwoman complained to her mother, "I feel so humiliated. I feel like I've been beaten up, like they kicked me." Her mom turned to her and said, "Think of every kick as a boost and you'll have it made." She never forgot.

We are going to tell you about someone who finally became president of the United States. At thirty-one, he failed in his first business, and a year later he was defeated in a legislative race. At thirty-four he failed in his second business. A year later the love of his life died, and at the age of thirty-five he was so destroyed that he had a nervous breakdown. At thirty-eight he lost another election and at forty-three lost a congressional race. He lost another congressional race at age forty-six and again at forty-eight. But he ran again when most would have given up. When he was fifty-five he lost a senatorial race and then, a year later, lost the race to become vice-president. Two years later, at age fifty-eight, he lost his second attempt at getting into the United States Senate.

Finally, at age sixty, he was elected president of the United States and led the country through one of the roughest eras in its history, the Civil War. His name was Abraham Lincoln.

It is at the moment of or shortly following an event that an internal decision or program is made and filed. It is a matter of a kind of attitude, in other words the angle or viewpoint from which we are in the habit of viewing life, and what movie is being shown to us on our screen called life. If Lincoln had paid attention to his failures he would have thought he was a failure. He obviously reframed his experiences and looked at them as times of learning and growing.

If you are born with a strong Aries imprint, you can, as mentioned in chapter 1, see this zodiac sign's "negatives" as "positives." That's right. Your "impulsiveness" becomes "quick reflexes." Your "arrogance" becomes "persistence in the face of obstacles."

It is a question of positioning your lens of perception, deciding what you're going to focus on. The storm of life is ever present with us. Think for a moment about your past. Perhaps you can even take a few extra minutes and roll the movie of your entire life from your earliest memories up to the present moment.

As you probably saw, there always have been storms in your life. Well, we have some good news about storms. Ship captains trained in handling hurricanes and cyclones head for the *eye of the storm,* the *center of the cyclone.*

Amazing as it might seem, in the middle of nature's violence is this area of complete calm, while all around it are dark clouds, winds, rains, and frightening waves. The calm eye of Hurricane Gilbert, the devastating storm of 1988, was eight miles in diameter!

So the real question becomes Where do you want home base to be? Where do you want to reside while making decisions or taking action? Do you like being caught up in the storm and becoming what is called in the East "The Wave-Tossed Man" or the "Drunken Monkey," being tossed here and there, up and down, by fate and circumstances, or do you want to reside in the center of your cyclone of life, in the calm peaceful eye of the storm, and handle things from there?

Believe it or not, some people prefer the former, the roller coaster. In the Chinese book of changes called the *I Ching,* which has been traced back to at least 1150 B.C., are sixty-four essays or hexagrams of advice on how to live a balanced life. In a sense they are sixty-four metaholograms of life. In number sixty-one, entitled "Inner Truth," there is a line of advice for the seeker that states,

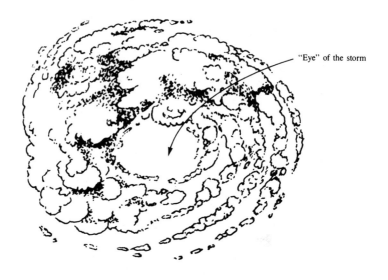

"Eye" of the storm

Satellite view of hurricane in
northern hemisphere

TOP VIEW

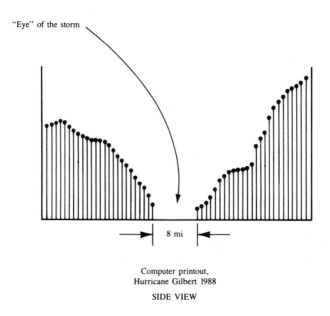

"Eye" of the storm

8 mi

Computer printout,
Hurricane Gilbert 1988

SIDE VIEW

Figure 4. The calm in the eye of the storm.

"You depend upon your external relationships to dictate your mood or to gauge your confidence in yourself. This can sometimes elevate you to the heights of joy or banish you to the depths of despair. Possibly you may enjoy such a range in emotion." As you see, the *I Ching* makes no judgment as to one's personal preference.

Facing the stark reality of life isn't always pleasant. It can sometimes be difficult. But even in the worst of human circumstances we have the choice of viewpoint. To assuage the fatalists who may be reading this book, let's say that in circumstances where we don't seem to have any control over *events* in our lives—the *what* of it—our free will *is* exercised in the *how* of it. We do control how we choose to experience life and what we are going to do with the information life gives us, no matter how disappointing or depressing.

There are thousands of examples of this from personal life accounts of those who have faced tragedy and severe handicaps in their lives. I am going to take the extreme example of what is one of the most physically, emotionally, and spiritually devastating situations in which human beings could have found themselves, one of the most anti-life environments mankind has ever created: death camps.

There have been a number of books describing personal accounts and research with survivors of the camps. One of the best books on the subject, written by Bruno Bettelheim, is *The Informed Heart*. As a psychiatrist in a death camp, he was fascinated by those who kept an open heart despite the unfathomable evil.

In a *New Realities* magazine article (July/August 1988), Dr. Blair Justice, award-winning author and researcher and professor of psychology at the University of Texas health science center, writes about the latest findings on how stress is handled by the attitude of the experiencer.

> The devastating effects of the Nazi concentration camps have been discussed for decades, but not much attention was given for a long time to the question, "How did anyone keep going and survive such stress?" Psychiatrist Joel Dimsdale, then at Stanford University School of Medicine, located 19 such survivors in the San Francisco area who were in relatively good health, and he subsequently identified the survivors' beliefs and appraisals as the source of their successful coping

methods. For instance, a number of the survivors learned to "focus on the good"—which meant being thankful for getting through the food line without a beating, or appreciating the sunset against the distant fields.

The former captives also benefited from focusing on a purpose for survival. Some survived to be reunited with their families, others to bear witness to the world of the atrocities, still others to seek revenge. A number kept from being defeated by retaining a sense of mastery or autonomy over some corner of their lives. They persisted in observing Yom Kippur in the face of all odds. They learned to congratulate themselves on just staying alive in a place whose very purpose was to kill everyone.

. . . How aversive or damaging an event is depends on how we choose to take it. . . . All these studies suggest that hardship, difficulty, even danger cannot be equated with distress and increased risk of illness. The adversity we face does not determine our physical or psychological arousal, our health or disease. How we interpret the situation and cope with it is what counts.[2]

The situation of stress can be imagined or real; the effect is the same. Perception is our reality, at least as far as the body is concerned, and we will be going into that shortly in greater detail.

This lens of perception you choose to focus on in the world is the point of the story of the lady and the tiger. There is no right answer. Your answer reflects whether or not you have a core belief that the universe is basically good (the glass half full). Your answer will give you an insight into your deepest belief concerning your feelings about the nature of life and your general attitude or frame—trust or distrust; optimism, or pessimism; a benevolent universe or God, or a random, chaotic, uncaring universe. No one can make that choice or decision except you. You.

TWO SYSTEMS, ONE MIND

We would like to introduce you to Lee Leftbrain and Robin Rightbrain, the two best vice-presidents of the biocomputer "corporation" of which you are the president and owner. You have assigned specific duties and functions to each, and each, in his or her own unique way, is essential to your full and complete functioning in life. Both are needed for the business of your living to be balanced.

Lee Leftbrain is the vice-president you have assigned to oversee certain areas of your concerns:

1. logic

2. sequential planning

3. rational analysis and decision making

4. use of language, except for jokes, puns, and idioms (Robin's department)

5. mathematics

6. linear, intellectual, nonemotional thinking

7. investigation of the whole by breaking it up into parts (in computer terms, digitization)

8. quality control—the person on the end of the assembly line who is paid to find mistakes and flaws

    Lee Leftbrain is the skeptic, the internal critic, the editor, who displays the "figure-figure" syndrome of constant thinking, and indulges in internal chatter. Lee uses approximately ten percent of the corporation's resources.

On the other side, specifically the right hemisphere, is Robin Rightbrain, also holding the title of vice-president of your corporation (corpus, meaning body) in charge of:

1. feelings and emotions

2. unexplainable intuitions

3. dreams—including daydreams, flying dreams, precognitive dreams, lucid dreams, resolution dreams

4. all parapsychological phenomena—including extrasensory perception, out-of-body experiences, near-death experiences, psychokinesis, bi-location, psychic healing, etc.

5. the elusive quality known as charisma or attractiveness

6. sexual energy (libido) and fantasies

7. personality

8. poetry and rich sensory descriptions of things

9. dance and rhythm

10. music

11. jokes, puns, and idioms

12. childlike or silly behavior

13. sudden personal insights, called the Ahh experience

14. sudden scientific breakthroughs or problem solving, called the Eureka experience

15. sudden, nonlogical compassion or sympathy

16. spiritual visions

17. praying

18. action through reproducing holographic thought pictures sent to the right brain

19. archetypes and metaphors

20. enthusiasm, passion

Robin uses approximately ninety percent of the corporation's resources.

Now that you are a little more familiar with the function of your two main employees in the biocomputer (mind), let's set up a little scenario. Imagine yourself sitting at the end of a long conference table. Last week you gave assignments to Lee Leftbrain and Robin Rightbrain to advise you about moving out of your present location and increasing your prosperity level. Should the move be to California or to Florida? They enter the room; Robin sits on your right, Lee on your left.

You ask Lee, full of nervous energy and dressed in a three-piece power suit with a tight collar, for the report and recommendations. Sitting with back straight up, military school style, Lee crisply opens an attaché case, takes out a thick, well-documented report with hundreds of computer printouts of cost analysis, and begins to read in a nonemotional, intellectual style, addressing you in a formal manner as Mr. or Ms.: "The R.O.I. has a three percent override of cost through a ten-year depreciation of the Fowler curve's estimates of loss of capital in a three-year termed deficiency mechanism of yield over 789.3 for 4.2 years depending on the coefficient factor analysis code 5 . . . blah blah blah. . . ." When finished, with hands folded, Lee remains at attention.

Then you turn to your right and ask Robin for a report. Robin appears very relaxed, feet up on the conference table, wearing jeans, sneakers, and a loose-fitting shirt. "Well," Robin answers, "I really don't know. As far as California is concerned, I understand the only culture they have is in yogurt." You both laugh. Lee does not. "Anyway, I just have a gut feeling that California would be the place to move to. Don't know why, it's just the way I feel. As a matter of fact, a few nights ago I had a dream that you were in California, in a swimming pool full of hundred-dollar bills. You sure looked happy! "

Most people have an internal conflict in their minds. They feel one way even though they know logically that they shouldn't. Their intuition tells them to do one thing when rationally it seems a mistake. Dr. Elmer E. Green, a director in the research department of the Menninger Foundation and a pioneer in biofeedback and voluntary control of internal states, in an enlightening book called *Ancient Wisdom and Modern Science*, writes,

> This left-right disparity is not limited in its effects to interhemispheric problems; it also can cause interpersonal trouble. For instance, my intensely left-brained father was often wrong, but for exactly correct reasons. And my intensely right-brained mother was often right, but for the wrong reasons. You can imagine how that worked. Though it caused trouble in the family, it gave me an excellent opportunity to become the family mediator, and for several years I had valuable experience in healing rational-intuitive splits, my own as well as those in the family. . . . The functional parts of the nervous system are not "hard wired," or unchangeable. Because they are instead plastic, normally unconscious habits of body, emotions, and mind can be reprogrammed in brain structures by self-regulation training, plus your own volition.

(In Futureshaping Technologies™ we call self-regulation training *holographic programming*, and volition is seen as attention, the activator of internal thoughts and pictures.)

So there you have it. Your two top vice-presidents have given you their reports. Who is right? Who makes the final decision? Yes, *you!*

You are the president and owner of the corporation. You, the spirit inhabiting the body, use the biocomputer mind as a *tool.*

Information is just information. In a way, all of your senses give you disinformation; they lie. Your feelings can lie, your eyes can be fooled, your hearing can be fooled, your smell can be fooled, and your taste can be fooled. Neurologically we never experience anything directly. Our minds just interpret the digital signals coming in through our senses. It's second hand. That's the way it has to be. If the information coming in through the environment were not censored, we would be overwhelmed, everything would come in with equal significance and we would be living in a blooming, buzzing confusion, hardly able to get a grip on reality.

SUMMARY

1. You are a spirit in a body with a control system called the mind.

2. Your mind is like a biocomputer, an information storage and retrieval system.

3. Your mind takes pictures like a movie camera. They are a special type of picture called holograms.

4. Holograms are three-dimensional pictures that record everything you see, hear, feel, smell, and taste at the time of the memory.

5. Information is equally distributed throughout a hologram. If it is broken into tiny pieces, you still get the whole picture.

6. Your mind is the control panel or switchboard between you the spirit and the body.

7. You are not your mind, you are the spirit viewing or looking at the information on your internal screen. If you were your mind, you wouldn't be able to see it.

8. The mind has two parts, two different lenses that focus on different information in the enviroment and body. One part (Lee) is analytical and rational, the other (Robin) is feeling and intuitive.

9. *Attention* is your power, the magic wand. Whatever memory or environmental stimulus you pay attention to increases. Whatever you pay attention to is what you are aware of, becomes the reality for you no matter

what is going on around you. Pay attention to what you don't have or what you view as deficits, and you will feel lacking and negative, perhaps even bitter and cynical. Pay attention to the miracles already happening in your life, and you will feel blessed.

NOTES

1. Reported by Marc McCutcheon in *Omni* Vol. 5 (Feb. 1983).
2. Blair Justice, *New Realities* (July/August 1988) and *Who Gets Sick—Thinking and Health*, (Houston: Peak Press, 1987).

Whatever you can do or dream you can do, begin it.
Boldness has genius, power and magic in it.
JOHANN WOLFGANG VON GOETHE

Relaxation and visualization are natural skills you use every day, whether you realize it consciously or not. This combination has many names: creative visualization, daydreams, meditation, self-hypnosis, autogenic training, progressive relaxation, and even, in some cases, praying.

It has a profound effect upon our lives. It has an immediate, amazing effect on our body and our self-image and it has an astonishing effect upon the quality, the enjoyment, and connected-ness of the moment-to-moment experience of our lives. Now, in the 1980s, there have been major breakthroughs in understanding this process: scientific experiments have proven that the mental images we hold in our mind affect the body immediately, down to the very cell structure.

The principles covered have started to become common knowledge. In the November 7, 1988, issue of *Newsweek*, the cover story was titled "Body and Soul." The subtitle read, "New discoveries linking the brain to the immune system suggest that state of mind can affect us right down to our cells" and it stated

> solid data connecting good thoughts to good health, or bad ones to falling ill, are still hard to come by. But lately, the doubts have begun to fade. The past ten years have witnessed an explosion of research findings suggesting that the mind and body act on each other in often remarkable ways . . . one study headed by psychologist Sandra Levy at the Pittsburgh Cancer Institute this year found that a factor called "joy"— meaning mental resilience and vigor—was the second strongest predictor of survival time for a group of patients with recurrent breast cancer. . . . The immune system seems to behave almost as if it had a brain of its own . . . [responding to] perceived social support and the way a patient coped with stress.
>
> The idea that thinking well helps make you well is becoming a truism in American medicine, and mind-body clinics are now offering therapies for everything from headaches to cancer. . . . Dr. Steven Locke, associate director of the Psychiatry Consultation Service at Boston's Beth Israel Hospital, calls the mind-body movement the "third revolution" in Western medicine—ranking it alongside the advent of surgery and the discovery of penicillin.
>
> The least controversial of the new behavioral therapies are those aimed at problems like insomnia, migraine headaches, ulcers, colitis and high blood pressure. In the Mind/Body Clinic at Boston's New England Deaconess Hospital, Dr. Herbert Benson introduces people with such stress-related disorders to the "relaxation response"—a serene state he describes as the physiological flip side to the "fight or flight" response. Benson has his patients sit quietly, close their eyes and concentrate on a short word or phrase for

a period of 10 to 20 minutes. Those who perform this simple exercise regularly will become "less angry, less depressed, less hostile, and less anxious." . . . 80 per cent of the patients were able to reduce either their blood pressure or their drug dosage.

Mind-body therapies are also widely accepted as treatments for pain. Hypnosis, for example, is so potent a pain-killer that physicians have used it as a substitute for anesthesia in surgery. Just as a person reading a magazine may become oblivious to sensations in his back, the Stanford psychiatrist David Spiegal wrote last year, a patient in a hypnotic trance can become unaware of pain by focusing on some other sensation or imagining that the painful area has been made numb. A hypnotized patient may experience a surgeon's scalpel as a "pencil being drawn lightly across his chest," he says, "and may remain free of pain even after emerging from the trance."

So as you do the astrological visualizations and attunements that you will be learning, you are releasing the positive aspects of your mind, heart, and body. You may also begin to experience other positive changes.

In most astrology books and tapes, there is a certain concentration on the negative traits. As you are beginning to realize now, if you pay attention to them, you will become them. If you cultivate your pessimism by visualizing the negative—failures, mistakes, faults—it will increase. You might say this is all Pollyanna, but science writer Daniel Goleman, in a 1987 *New York Times* article entitled "Research Affirms Power of Positive Thinking," says

Pollyanna was right, new research shows.

Optimism—at least reasonable optimism—can pay dividends as wide-ranging as health, longevity, job success and higher scores on achievement tests.

The new research is an outgrowth of earlier work on the power of self-fulfilling prophecies. That early work concentrated largely on how individuals tend to conform to others' expectations of them, a phenomenon known as the "Pygmalion effect." If anything, researchers have found, the Pygmalion effect is more pervasive than has been thought. The new work looks at people's expectations about their own lives and finds that the power of expectations goes beyond mere achievement to visceral, emotional qualities.

"Our expectancies not only affect how we see reality but also affect reality itself," according to Edward E. Jones, a psychologist at Princeton University, who reviewed the research on expectancy in a recent issue of *Science*.

Another example of the power of relaxed visualization is from Australian psychologist Alan Richardson. He wanted to see if physical skills could be improved with visualization practice, so he took three groups of basketball players and tested the ability of each group to make free throws. Each day he had Group A practice shooting free throws for twenty minutes. Group B was instructed not to practice. Now Group C was a different story. He had them spend twenty minutes a day visualizing themselves shooting perfect baskets.

As you have probably already guessed, the no-practice group, Group B, showed no improvement. Group A improved twenty-four percent. Group C, just through the power of visualization, improved twenty-three percent, almost as much as the group that practiced. Now you understand why American, Russian, and other Olympic teams have been teaching their athletes these methods.

Remember Roger Bannister? The so-called experts of the day believed it was impossible for a human being to run the mile in under four minutes. Bannister imagined he could, and he did! Of course, once other runners knew it was possible, they too began running the mile under four minutes.

Some of the most important research in the United States on using visualizations for peak performance in all areas of life—business, sports, and personal—is being conducted by Dr. Charles A. Garfield. Garfield was a team member of NASA's historic Apollo moon landing and is the president of the Performance Sciences Institute in Berkeley, California. He interviewed hundreds of professionals in the sports and business fields and asked them to describe the way they felt. Then he compiled these reports into several hundred words.

The following description is how you can feel through relaxation techniques and mental rehearsal using visualizations, to be on a roll in your life:

> All at once it seems as though everything is working for me. There is no sense of needing to do anything. My actions unfold as they do in pleasant dreams, though my body may be putting out great efforts. I have no thoughts about what I should do or how I should do it. Everything is happening automatically, as though I have tuned myself in on a radio beam that directs my nervous system so that it works in synchronization with everything in and around me. I feel insulated from all distractions. Time disappears, and even though I know the speed of actions taking place around me, I feel I have all the time I need to respond accurately and well. I am so completely involved in the action that there is not even a question of confidence or the lack of it.
>
> There are no issues such as worries about failure or feelings of fatigue. Even such feelings as momentary fear appear to serve me, changing automatically into positive forces.... I am acutely aware of colors, sounds, the presence of people around me, the feeling of being a source of power and energy in this moment in time. It is a trance-like state, and I feel ... as though the usual barriers between me and the outside world have been pulled away, and I am completely at one with myself and the physical world with which I am interacting. It is a wonderful feeling, crisp, full of joy, more *real* than the everyday world, going very deep.

In his book, *Peak Performance, Mental Training Techniques of the World's Greatest Athletes*, Garfield states,

> Without a doubt, the most dramatic contribution to the advancement of goal-setting skills in recent years has been the Soviets' introduction of visualization. Use of this skill substantially increased the effectiveness of goal-setting, which up to then

had been little more than a dull listing procedure. As used in goal-setting, visualization is a refinement of mental rehearsal techniques developed by the Russians. During mental rehearsal, athletes create mental images of the exact movements they want to emulate in their sport. The Soviets found that mental images act as precursors in the process of generating neuromuscular impulses, which regulate and control physical movement. These images are holographic (three dimensional) and function primarily at the subliminal level. The holographic imaging mechanism enables you to quickly solve spatial problems such as assembling a complex machine, choreographing a dance routine, or running visual images of plays through your mind. The mental images act as three-dimensional blueprints for encoding the information required to effect exact sequences and ranges of physical movement in athletic activity. In the process of goal-setting, we create detailed mental images of actions and desired outcomes—a phenomenon that is still being studied. According to researchers, we enhance and accelerate our physical learning process by combining mental imagery and physical training.

Dr. Garfield reports that

In my meetings with the Soviet researchers in Milan, they discussed government-funded athletic programs that integrate sophisticated mental training and rigorous physical training. One study evaluating these intensive programs suggests their potential. Four matched groups of world-class Soviet athletes diligently trained for many hours each week. The training regimens were as follows:

Group 1—100 percent physical training

Group 2—75 percent physical training, 25 percent mental training

Group 3—50 percent physical training, 50 percent mental training

Group 4—25 percent physical training, 75 percent mental training

When the four groups were compared shortly before the 1980 Winter Games in Lake Placid, Group 4 had shown significantly greater improvement than Group 3, with Groups 2 and 1 following, in that order.

Startling results, don't you think?

*

Dr. Michael Samuels, M.D., author of *Seeing With the Mind's Eye: The History, Techniques, and Uses of Visualization*, reports on the medical uses of the placebo effect. This phenomenon occurs when plain sugar pills or other nonpharmaceutical substances are prescribed by a doctor for a patient as a cure for illness. Because the patient believes in the ritual of the prescription and has faith in Western medicine, cures take place with startling regularity. Dr. Samuels also used distilled water to cure peptic ulcers and colored dye to cure warts. Some experiments have shown sixty, seventy, even eighty percent cure rates for headaches, backaches, and so on, even though there was no reason why the sugar pills should have brought about this apparent cure.

It seems to follow, then, that if a large percentage of people can heal themselves with a placebo, there must be, deep inside ourselves, some sort of switch we turn on that heals us. No one has yet discovered what or where it is located, yet researchers know it is there, and are just now beginning to discover how it works. We really don't need to know why it works, what is important is how it works. For example, scientists still don't know exactly *why* electricity works. Theories differ depending on whom you ask. The important thing is they know *how* it works, thereby enabling us to put it to use.

Frankly, it doesn't matter whether everything we've reported so far is scientific fact, discovered by Nobel Prize-winning scientists, or not. The only thing that really matters is, *does it work for you?* After learning the easy methods of relaxing and visualizing we will be telling you about, does the quality of your life improve? Do you have more love? Are you more relaxed and is there less stress? Do you have more fun and more enjoyment out of every minute of the day? Do you have more patience and understanding? Are you more productive?

WHY RELAXED VISUALIZATIONS WORK

One of the reasons relaxed visualizations have such a powerful influence on our lives is *because the body doesn't know the difference between what is real or imagined.* Think of that for a moment. The body accepts both as the same and responds appropriately. Nightmares are a good example of what we are talking about. If we dream we are being chased by a hungry tiger, it makes no difference whether there really is one in our bedroom or whether we just imagined there is. Our body will react *as if* there is one there and will begin sweating. The heart will begin beating faster, blood vessels will contract, adrenaline and other biochemicals will enter the blood stream. The body will manifest all of the biophysical changes that accompany true fear, even if there isn't really a tiger in the room.

Sex dreams are another example. Regardless of whether or not there really is another person lying beside us in bed, if we dream, imagine, or fantasize (all similar states of visualization), we will still experience all the feelings of sexual arousal, sometimes even climaxing in our dreams.

*

If we could get you to imagine a hot and humid summer day now, and perhaps to see yourself arriving home and going into your kitchen to make yourself a tall glass of lemonade, then perhaps you might even be able to hear the ice cubes dropping into the glass, the gurgle of the water. Then you cut the lemon in half and squeeze the juice into the glass. Just the right amount, and before you put the lemon half down you lick it....

*

Well, how's your mouth? Did it pucker, salivate? Remembering your favorite dinner will cause your body to secrete digestive enzymes even if there is no food anywhere in the vicinity.

Dr. Karl Pribram, whom we mentioned earlier, is famous for his findings about how the mind forms pictures, how it influences thinking and how our very neurology is affected by it. He says that when we imagine something with rich sensory details (what it looks like, what the sounds are, what one is feeling at the time, the smell, the taste) it sets up a *neurological template*, a set of instructions to our mind and body. In a sense, what we imagine or dream of becomes our rudder through life.

REPROGRAMMING THE BIOCOMPUTER

Before we start talking about reprogramming old beliefs and personal programs that keep us from being the best we can be, from operating in the state of peak performance, let us say that you already know how to do this, even if you can't put it into words. It is a natural, built-in tool of the mind and body. You may not have gotten an operator's manual when you were born, but it is built in there.

When you were born, your biocomputer was open to programming. If you are like most people, your mother was the one to start giving you programs about how to live life, according to the information she had about what was appropriate. Maybe she programmed into you that you should brush your teeth three times a day, wash behind the ears, always wear clean underwear in case you get into a car accident and have to go to the hospital, never have sex before marriage, and so on. Well, sometime during adolescence, if not before, you consciously or subconsciously began to go through the holographic programs given to you by your mother, father, teachers, friends, and relatives. Some of the implanted programs or beliefs you kept, the others you somehow de-wired. You still have the memories of the old programs, but somehow you defused their command value. You might still see your mother yelling at you to stay within the speed limits, but that doesn't keep you there. Other beliefs still have a hold on you, command over you, have mastered you.

So now you know you already have the ability to program or deprogram any of your memories or belief systems, even before we give you the latest formulas. You might ask why, if you already have that ability, you are not doing it, but that is a question for another book.

First, to consciously reprogram or activate your highest potential you need to get your mind into an alpha-theta state. There are four brain waves now known:

> **Delta**—0 to 4 cycles per second (cps), the slowest,
> during deep sleep

Theta — 4 to 8 cps, deep reverie, almost near sleep, but not fully sleeping

Alpha — 8 to 13 cps, relaxed yet aware, eyes open or closed

Beta — 13 to 26 cps, our normal waking, thinking, active state

These may be scientific terms, but let me assure you that you go through each of these states daily. Even though we are going to give you techniques for entering these states, you already do so naturally every day. For example, when you are going to sleep at night and are not fully asleep but not fully awake, you are in alpha-theta. When you awaken in the morning, not asleep, nor yet fully awake or up and out of bed, you are in alpha-theta. Anytime you catch yourself daydreaming during the day, fantasizing, or fixating on an object like a flower or book, you are in that same magical brain-wave state, also called the hypnagogic state.

WHAT IS SELF-HYPNOSIS?

The term is derived from Hypnos, the name of the Greek god of sleep. The word hypnosis is misleading because it really has less to do with sleep than it does with relaxation and pleasant daydreams.

Much of the credit for taking hypnosis out of the dark ages and restoring it to good standing goes to Dr. Milton Erickson. Erickson was the psychiatrist who was to a great extent responsible for the AMA re-recognizing hypnosis as "a valuable therapeutic adjunct."

In the early days of Western medicine, before modern anesthesia, hypnosis was used to perform thousands of operations and, other than alcohol, was the only anesthetic available. It still is used as the only anesthetic in many operations today. Dr. Alexander Levitan, a cancer specialist at Unity Medical Center in Fridley, Minnesota, for example, has "used hypnosis in 21 major operations. These included gallbladder removal, caesarean section, hysterectomy, and a four and a half hour operation in which a patient's jawbone was sawed apart. Only two had to be switched to regular anesthetic," reported *105 Magazine*.

In an article that appeared in *Esquire* magazine in January 1983, Thomas Morgan wrote about how he learned self-hypnosis to help him overcome a writing block. Morgan was so successful that he began to research this amazing tool that is making such a fantastic comeback in the last decade. Much of the renewed interest is due to the work of Dr. John Grinder and Richard Bandler, founders of Neuro-Linguistic Programming, who have popularized Erickson's work and made the tools of self-transformation so easily available to the average person.

Morgan wrote,

> How shall I describe self-hypnosis? I don't want to exaggerate. For one thing, it is a temporary, self-managed altered state of consciousness that can make the resources of your brain and body and persona more responsive to your needs. Looked at another way, self-hypnosis is a natural phenomenon that helps you follow your own suggestions, listen to your own admonitions, and submit to your own commands (Isn't that what you've always wanted to do?) just as the hypnotized subject in a one-to-one clinical session responds to the authority of a professional hypnotist during and after a trance. In self-hypnosis, you are *both* subject and hypnotist . . . a technique that most people can learn in minutes and practice for a lifetime. . . . Think of it! . . . Self-hypnosis, folks, is cheap, healthy, painless, and useful, and it travels well through space and time. Moreover, it feels good.

> In hypnosis, you are wide-awake but focused within yourself. It is not a waking dream—a *working* dream would be more like it, a kind of businesslike hyper-consciousness that lets you concentrate, really concentrate, on a matter of importance without mumbo jumbo at the beginning or rigmarole at the end, and all under *your* control.

> That is the point. Psychiatrists like to describe the event in hypnosis as a trance. I accept the word, but it is misleading, because it describes the event only from the observer's viewpoint. To most people, *trance* probably suggests a spaced-out person dropping out or away from reality, letting go, tending toward zero—whereas to you, in your trance, inside *your* head, you are in a vivid state of concentrated awareness. You are still in the real

world working on a real problem. You are in charge.

In general usage, the word *trance* misses that sense of direction. It suggests *less* control when, in your experience, it may mean that you have more command over your life than ever before. It can, I believe, connect your unconscious to your problems. And if, either within the trance or soon after, you find new ideas, new combinations of old ideas, unexpected twists of thought, or simply more courage to go on, you will know hypnosis has been working.

The best definition of self-hypnosis we have been able to come up with is a pleasant and relaxed interruption of a person's normal hectic pace in order to turn the healing and creative problem-solving aspects of attention on themselves before engaging again in their normal activities—refreshed, replenished, and renewed. In a sense, it's like taking a bath in grace.

SELF-HYPNOSIS AND RELAXATION TECHNIQUES

The first step in holographic self-hypnosis is learning how to make the mind and body relaxed and receptive to whatever positive holograms and visualizations you choose to use. Here are some easily learned techniques. Try them all, find the one you like the best, and practice it three times a day for a week or two. Trust that you'll know when you can enter the alpha/theta/daydreaming state at will. We suggest one of the three times be at night, as you are falling asleep, because this will help reinforce the technique. Perhaps the other two times could be midmorning and midafternoon when you need a pick-me-up. Remember, it is not the length of time you practice, but the frequency. Five to seven minutes a session is adequate, though many people prefer more.

You need only practice until you are able to reach the self-hypnosis state at will under any stressful situations, usually after about two weeks. Then, as in learning to ride a bike, you won't have to practice any more; it will just come naturally whenever you need it.

When you have accomplished this, you can use your astrological visualizations and attunements, whether you have created your own using the material in this book or purchased premade tapes. You can also have a friend or family member read the visualizations and attunements to you from this book while you are relaxed and thinking of a pleasant place, like a beach. Remember, since your body doesn't know the difference between what is real or imagined, if you visualize that you are on a beach, after a few minutes your neurology begins to react as if it really were. So in a sense you are having what I call a minivacation. Bon voyage! Enjoy yourself!

BASIC RELAXATION
AND VISUALIZATION TECHNIQUES

TAKE A HOT BATH   Hot baths quickly relax a person and promote good blood circulation. Lock the door and put a "Do Not Disturb" sign on it, or let the family know that you need thirty minutes of private time. Bring your battery-operated tape recorder in to play your "Change Your Destiny" tapes, write letters, or write in your journal or diary.* You might buy yourself a bathtub shelf that goes across the width of the tub (a wide board will do) and gives you a space for books, pad, candles, and so on.

PROGRESSIVE RELAXATION   This method was developed by Dr. Edmund Jacobson, an American physician, whose research into muscle physiology and relaxation gained him worldwide fame and set the groundwork for other psychotherapeutic techniques, natural childbirth techniques, and new methods of treating tension-related diseases such as high blood pressure. Similar methods have been practiced for hundreds of years in yoga and other such disciplines. Here is the basic technique:

Sit down in a comfortable chair or lie down on a bed or couch. Again try to take any precautions necessary to make sure you are not disturbed. You are going to progressively tense and relax your whole body, starting with your feet and then moving up your body through the major muscle groups. Take a deep breath, let it out, and tense your foot muscles slightly (not too much because feet

---

* Mary Orser and Richard A. Zarro, along with musicians Dr. Karl Hans Berger and Vinnie Martucci, have produced a special series of audiotapes designed to activate the potentials of your personal resources. For information about these "Change Your Destiny" tapes or other Futureshaping technologies, seminars, lectures, and training, write Futureshaping Technologies Incorporated, Post Office Box 489, Woodstock, NY 12498.

and calves are prone to cramps) and hold for a count of three. Then relax. Tighten again, then relax. Do it a third time, then leave the foot relaxed and move up to the calf muscles. Tighten and relax three times, the third time leaving the calves relaxed at the end. Then, tensing and relaxing in sets of three, move up to the thighs, then the stomach muscles. Tighten your hands and arms three times each and then relax, letting them go limp on your armrest or thighs as you proceed to the neck and shoulder area. After that, tense your face and neck muscles as if you were playing with a child and making a monster face. This part of the progressive relaxation technique is often featured in men's and women's magazines as a way to keep the face young looking and wrinkle free. Yoga has a similar exercise for the face and neck called the lion's roar for obvious reasons.

Now you have reached the last area, your eyes. This you can start with eyes open or closed, depending on your personal preference. Tighten and relax the eyes three times and then, after the third and final time, leave the eyes relaxed. By that time, you will be in a relaxed state and can either put on your visualization tape, have someone read to you in a slow, melodic voice, or do other visualization techniques that will be described later.

THE BREATH TECHNIQUE   Sit or lie down in a safe and comfortable place and arrange not to be disturbed. When you sit down, unbutton or untie anything that is tight or restrictive on your body. Close your eyes and concentrate on breathing in through your nose and out through your mouth. Feel the air coming in your nostrils and feel the air against your lips going out. Listen to the sound and the rhythm. Inhale slowly and deeply, pause a moment, then exhale slowly and completely, allowing your stomach to rise and fall as you breathe. In a few minutes you will feel more calm, comfortable, and relaxed, and your breathing will become slower and even.

THE ONE-SPOT TECHNIQUE   Sitting or prone, pick a spot in front of you and keep looking at it as you blink your eyes twelve times. Afterwards, when you close your eyelids, they will feel relaxed and tired. This relaxed sensation will spread through to the rest of your body in pleasant waves.

MENTAL PICTURES OF RELAXATION   This technique may be the easiest of all. It works because you have previously conditioned yourself for relaxation by experiencing it some time in the past. In this technique all you do is get into a comfortable position and remember back to a time in your life when you felt safe, secure, calm, and relaxed. Holding the scene or object in your mind, using all your senses, that is, what it looked like, what it sounded like, what it felt like or smelled like, will *automatically* relax the body. It's called a *conditioned response.* You can use anything you have experienced, read, or seen in movies or on television, or even pictures from magazines. For instance, you can imagine sitting by a stream on a perfect fall day and just happening to see a leaf begin to fall to the ground, slowly, back and forth.

SIMPLE BREATH RELAXATION As you begin to take slow, deep breaths, see yourself exhaling tension and stress. You can visualize this as a color that represents the negative for you. Then inhale calm and peace, seeing in the incoming air the color that represents relaxation and healing for you. Your favorite color is a good one to start with.

Another way, as you breathe easily and naturally, is to repeat over and over a word of your choice at the exhalation. Many people have found great success with the simple word *one,* because it has no distracting connotations. Other words commonly chosen are *relax, peace, love,* and *light.* If you have any distracting thoughts, just visualize them as a bubbles on a stream of fast-moving clouds drifting by from your left to your right and out of sight, returning to your chosen word.

PARACHUTING INTO PARADISE
Various Deepening Techniques and the Creation of an Internal Sanctuary or Visualization Room

Once you get yourself to this relaxation state, called *alpha,* you can turn on your visualization tape or otherwise return to your reprogramming.

You might be interested in achieving even deeper states of relaxation and exploring the use of an internal screening room for your visualizations. If so, let's first go into a few techniques to deepen your state of relaxation. The most commonly used is the elevator technique. After you have achieved a certain depth of relaxation, you can deepen it easily by imagining that you are standing in front of an elevator, and the elevator door opens. You enter, the door closes, and you watch the numbers of the floors above the door lighting up as the elevator descends. Now you see that the number ten is lit up. Feel the elevator taking you down to deeper and deeper levels of comfort. Now you watch the number nine light up. You are deeper and even more relaxed than you already were. See the number eight light up. You are deeper still. Now seven. Then six. Deeper still. five ... four ... three ... two ... one. You are now much more relaxed and comfortable, and your mind is in a more open and receptive frame.

Before we go on to the next step, let us give you several other options to use if you don't like the image of the elevator. Some people prefer using stairs, counting down from ten to one just as in the elevator technique. You could also see yourself *parachuting down into paradise*, floating and counting from ten to one until you land gently on the ground.

We always encourage people to make up their own techniques or images. Personalizing it seems to give it more power. None of the previous suggestions worked for a client of ours, and we suggested she come up with her own. After several days of experimenting she developed the technique of seeing herself rolling down a gentle hill, through a magical hole in a hedge. It doesn't matter *why* that particular image worked for her, just as long as it worked.

The next step after deepening your level of relaxation is to create for yourself a sort of private room, internal sanctuary, or private laboratory. You'll only need to do this once, and from then on, after using your deepening technique, you'll automatically go to this special space. There are many different labels for our inner viewing room: the *center*, the *private workshop*, the *power point*, the *safe place*, the *eye of the storm*. It doesn't really matter what you call it, or where you put it. Some people even choose to visualize it outdoors, like a favorite beach or mountain waterfall.

All that's required is that you return time and time again to the same place and that you have some sort of screen on which to watch your visualization, or a stage on which to watch it being acted out. Make it as relaxed, comfortable, safe, and secure a setting as possible.

SHAPE YOUR FUTURE BY MAKING A MOVIE

Now you are ready to visualize on the blank screen, a bare stage. The basic technique is to create a movie for yourself. You are the star! You are the director and producer! *The key is to see yourself as already being in the desired state, having achieved what you want.* When you are constructing the movie, pay attention to details, filling the movie with rich sensory data. See, hear, and feel yourself as healthy, attractive, slim, self-confident, successful, at that sales presentation, the public-speaking engagement, the important dinner party . . . whatever you choose. It is not necessary to know *how* what you are asking for is going to happen, just to see yourself having already attained it.

Once you have the movie just the way you want it, putting in as many people as you can (like throwing a party celebrating your new promotion with your friends), begin to run the movie on your screen or see it on the stage. You're going to watch it three times. The first two times, watch it as the audience. The third and final time, you are *acting it out*, no longer just watching yourself act it out. Each time pay relaxed attention to how you are standing, the tone of your voice, how you feel in the state of already having the thing you desire.

After that, simply reverse the deepening technique you have chosen. Start counting slowly from one to ten, telling yourself that at ten your eyes will open and that in a few minutes you will feel refreshed, replenished, and rejuvenated, as if you had taken a three-hour nap. Using relaxation techniques to combat fatigue is one of the first applications Futureshaping Technologies™ teaches in executive stress management courses. You will be amazed by the results.

You may be wondering why you first look at yourself in your movie and then finally feel yourself *being* in it. Researchers have found actually being in it to have a more powerful effect on your neurology. For example, psychologists Georgia Nigro and Ulric Neisser of Cornell duplicated and expanded the experiments of Dr. Richardson's basketball free-throw research. They were interested in finding out which different types of visualization were most powerful. So they organized three groups of dart players. Group A was told not to practice. The people in group B visualized themselves throwing the darts at a board as if they were actually at the line throwing. They were looking out of their own eyes. Group C was instructed to watch themselves as if in a movie or video, seeing themselves throwing. The results were that groups B and C improved, while the no-practice group did not. The real surprise was that group B showed twice the improvement of group C.

Most of all, remember that there is ultimately no "right way" to relax your body. It already knows how to do it. Just let it happen. There is no "correct" way to feel while it's happening. People experience a variety of sensations, everything from tingling, floating, radiating, and pulsing, to warmth, coolness, heaviness, or lightness in the limbs. Trust yourself and have *fun* playing with the various techniques. If it's not a pleasure, you might get far greater recreation, rejuvenation, and relaxation from doing something that is.

SUMMARY

1. Relaxation and visualization are natural skills you use every day, whether you realize it consciously or not. This combination has been called by many names: creative visualizations, daydreams, meditation, self-hypnosis, autogenic training, progressive relaxation, and praying.

2. The use of self-guided imagery and visualizations can change the very cells of our bodies almost instantaneously.

3. Visualizations of movements or mental rehearsal of situations without physical practice are almost as effective as the actual actions.

4. Placebo experiments prove that *you* have the power to heal yourself in many cases.

5. The reason visualizations work is because the body doesn't know the difference between what is real and what is imagined.

6. Act as if something were true and sooner or later it becomes so.

7. Visualizations set up a blueprint, a *neurological template*, a program of instructions for the body to follow.

8. You already know how to program and deprogram your belief systems and behavioral patterns.

9. A relaxed body leads to a relaxed mind. A relaxed mind leads to a relaxed body.

10. You owe it to yourself to have one place in the whole universe that is yours and yours alone, a place of security and serenity that is internal and can never be taken away from you.

11. To bring about any event or change in your life you wish, create and view a movie of yourself already having and enjoying it. Be, do, think, act, feel, dress, walk, talk, move, and gesticulate as if it had already occurred and the outside reality will, sooner or later, match your internal experience.

*The twelve signs of the Zodiac lay down twelve different
"paths" of life. . . . Every sign has its own manner of
expression, both in a higher and in a lower sense, and it
depends on the person himself which options he will take
and how he will use them.*

KAREN HAMAKER-ZONDAG, *Astro-Psychology*

The twelve-spoked wheel revolves around the Heavens.

Rig Veda (the most ancient collection of Hindu sacred verses)

✱

*The signs of the Zodiac are identified with . . . celestial
hierarchies of Cosmic Builders. These hierarchies constitute
collectively the Universal Mind, the operative creative
energy of the macrocosm. The Zodiac as a whole is a vast*

*cosmic lens focalizing upon the Earth the combined powers
of the hierarchies, thereby making of the Earth as a
whole, or of Man-in-the-whole, a microcosm.*

DANE RUDHYAR, *The Astrology of Personality*

✳

The night is especially starry. You look east to where one of the
zodiac signs is rising, then trace with your eyes the planets' path
overhead to where it disappears on the western horizon.

From your place at the hub of the heavens, you visualize the
twelve spokes of the zodiac wheel, seeing how they divide the territories of the twelve signs into pie-shaped sections, all pointing at
you. At any time half of them are in the sky and half are below the
horizon, unseen but felt through the body of Mother Earth. You
sense the energy of each sign as it rises in the east, culminates, and
then sets in the west. Deep in your memory you follow the rhythm
of this great turning wheel — a cycle that has taken place once for
every day of your life.

✳

The heavens are filled with cycles. The rotation of the Earth marks
the cycle of our days. Our Moon marks the months as it circles
around the Earth, and the Earth's revolution around the Sun marks
our years. There are longer and longer cycles, including many that
go beyond the span of our lifetime.

An important key to transforming cosmic patterns is an understanding of cycles.

As we have seen, the rhythms of plants, animals, and humans
keep pace with cosmic cycles. There are measurable changes in our
biological rhythms and observable changes in our psychological
responses at different times of the day, month, and year. Our
responses to longer cycles can also be observed as our lives go
through a succession of phases.

Astrological tradition divides the cycle into twelve phases — the
zodiac signs. From the Earth — our vantage point — the Sun, Moon,
and planets all travel around this "rim of the heavens," each at its
own speed. The Sun completes the cycle annually. Therefore it is
in the sky territory of each zodiac sign every year at the same season. Through the centuries a body of tradition has developed iden-

tifying the characteristics of each zodiac sign, and the imprint on a person born with the Sun in that sign.[1]

The Moon and planets, moving at their own speeds, can visit the signs of the zodiac at different times than the Sun, but even when, for instance, they visit the Aries sector in midwinter, they express, in their own ways, the *new beginning*, early spring energy characteristic of the Sun's annual visit from about March twentieth or twenty-first to April twentieth.[2]

The Moon goes through each sign in two and a half days—and, at the other end of the time scale, Pluto, the most distant and therefore slowest of the known planets, spends from twelve to thirty-one years in a sign.[3] Although the details of the sign descriptions have changed through the centuries, certain basic archetypal themes have remained constant. These themes seem to be built into the collective human unconscious. Each person carries the imprint of the whole zodiac and can express the themes of any of the signs. But certain signs in each horoscope are more strongly imprinted—such as the signs that the Sun and Moon were in and the sign on the eastern horizon (ascendant) at the time of birth.

Astrologers have noted that this reflection of zodiac signs emphasized at birth happens whether or not the person consciously knows of the traditions associated with these particular signs. This would fit with the theory that the signs are morphic fields. In fact, typical characteristics of a strongly imprinted sign can also be observed in the horoscopes of animals, and there are breeders who breed for certain zodiac sign characteristics, just as they breed for certain genetic characteristics.

No zodiac sign is, in itself, either good or bad. But, as illustrated earlier in connection with Aries, each has characteristics that can go either way—assets if used rightly, liabilities if misused.

All of us have exhibited negative manifestations of particular signs: the too-impulsive Aries; the overcritical Virgo; the Pisces lost in a dream world. . . .

All of us have also exhibited positive manifestations of particular signs: the Aries whose energy starts a good thing happening; the Virgo whose fine discrimination brings about something as nearly perfect as possible; the Pisces whose beautiful dream is expressed in our world of reality.

We could look at all of these as *habits in the morphic fields of the zodiac archetypes*. We recall Sheldrake's statement that "all organisms . . . are continuously recreating themselves under the influence of their own past states." It would seem that this includes both our personal habits of expressing astrological characteristics and the habits of our culture.

In other words, in this two-way flow, *you both express various habits of the archetypal field, and contribute to modification of the field by adding energy to certain of its expressions rather than others.*

We will give you how-to hints for tuning into the positive expressions of each zodiac sign. Also, as we have said, even though certain signs will be of special importance in your horoscope, each of us bears the imprint of the whole zodiac. Thus, we have available to us energy patterns that can balance out any seeming imbalance in our astrological expression.

You probably already know your sunsign, and after you read the section on it, you'll be glad you were born when you were. The sections on your moonsign and rising sign can also help you feel in tune with these aspects of your nature.

You can know the zodiac signs in the way you know different countries, each with its own spirit, ways of doing things, language, and interests. The following pages are about the positive, fulfilling expressions of the zodiac.

Astrological archetypes, like other archetypes, are best experienced by *tuning into their mythological themes.* Each of us is cast as an actor in one version or another of the story—in fact, it seems we contribute to the creation of our particular plots. All over the world people tune into archetypal consciousness by arts and music, dancing, enacting myths: rituals in which they picture themselves playing the parts of the mythic beings. In spiritual disciplines, consciousness is purified by visualizing—and identifying with—the archetype, not only as a whole being but also in fine detail: personality, appearance, way of moving, clothing, themes of a mythic being's life. Only when our mythic selves resonate with purer expressions of archetypal themes do we bring about positive changes in how the archetypes manifest.

All the purer archetypal themes are beautiful—what repels us is the incrustation of negative habits of expressing these themes, both cultural and individual.

We give you below some keys to the kingdom of each zodiac sign. These keys can open the way for you to reach its heart, to sense the rhythms, themes, and symbols of its energy, its colors and sounds, its gems, animals, and places, its recurring myths.

You increase your positive expressions of the sign's energies when you do such things as: wear clothing or look at objects that have the sign's colors and that please you; wear or carry its gems; eat with enjoyment a food associated with it; put up a poster of an associated place that you would like to visit.

To help you use the mythic key, we give you for each zodiac sign *visualizations* and an *attunement*.

The *first visualization*, the short one, connects you with the energy expressions of the particular phase in the growth cycle that the sign symbolizes.

The *second visualization* is a story that casts you in the role of a person expressing the sign's energies—acting out one version of the key myth. This visualization leads into the *attunement*, which is expressed in the first person, identifying your *I* with the *archetypal I.* The attunement could be considered an *invocation*—invoking the archetype.

It might be that you don't see yourself in the particular scenario we give for one of the zodiac signs. You can appreciate that the principal character is expressing themes of the sign, but it is not a specific role you can identify with. In this case, feel free to change any details you wish. For example, some of our visualizations have high-tech images. Maybe your mythic self doesn't connect to high-tech. You could then change the setting, the century, the cast of characters, the specific story plot—just keep to the basic themes.

At first it can be easier to stay in mythic awareness when you don't have to keep reminding yourself of the details. After you can tune more clearly into the archetype, then your mythic, or dream, self tells you its stories in vivid detail, from the pure monomyth to the most specific happening in your own life.

On the way to that state, it can free your consciousness from having to put in the details if you either use a cassette tape, or have someone read to you your visualization story and attunement, after you have achieved an open state (as described in chapters 3 and 4). To reinforce the effect you can imagine a movie of the story with you in the lead role (see chapter 4).

It is important that you work with these in ways that make you feel good. Focus on attributes and expressions of the sign for which you have an affinity. You will find, in the appendix, key words for each sign that will also help you understand its energies.

In your horoscope certain zodiac signs are emphasized in particular ways. But you sit at the hub of the wheel, related to all signs, and therefore you can benefit from tuning into the mythic realm of each one. You might wish to start with:

* *the signs most emphasized* in your horoscope, proceeding in any order you choose, at your own pace;
* *your sunsign,* then moving around the zodiac in sequence;
* *beginning of the growth cycle* (Capricorn);
* *beginning of the outward manifestation cycle* (Aries).

The visualizations we give are extremely effective for connecting you with the empowering energy of the sign. In addition, you will find in the appendix a list of key words for each zodiac sign. These words have been carefully chosen to help you understand the characteristics of the sign. We also give you key words for the other major astrological factors—planets, aspects, and houses, and we will be showing you how to put these key words together in sentences that describe the potentials of your astrological imprints.

One thing more—it is important to *stop giving energy to malfunctions of the zodiac signs.* Instead, change the subject with yourself, envisioning a positive expression of the particular energy.

The excitement and fun of what you are doing will open up your imagination on the levels of your being where the real changes can take place. Enjoy the adventure!

✳

ARIES VISUALIZATIONS

BREAKING THROUGH NEW GROUND. Deep in the heart of you pulse the heat and rich power of the fully awakened seed. Your roots are deep and strong, penetrating Mother Earth with a plunging, piercing power. Your sprout presses upward, pushing the stubborn heavy soil, toiling and thrusting with persistence, over and over, up, up, and, with a fiery power, it breaks through, severing the soil, sending your hope-green shaft above the underground into the warmth and light of the ruling sun.

✳

THE FIRST LANDING ON MARS. The excitement fills your entire body with an almost imperceptible tingling and moves up into your head with a wonderful euphoria—you see Mars, the fiery red planet, for the first time. It floats like a ruby in a sea of diamonds against the blue-black curtain of deep space. You speak to your crew and give orders to prepare the ship for landing.

You relax for a moment, staring at Mars through your view screen. It has been a long hard journey, but you loved being a pioneer, a survivor. You are going to be on the first landing craft. You want to be the first to put your foot down on the red dust of the Martian desert.

You have had other adventures in other places, but this gives you a charge of electric energy, a dream come true.

As you address the men and women of your landing party, a fiery zeal fills your heart and spirit. You are confident, assertive, and inspiring. All is ready for this new beginning.

The space lock opens and you step out, the first. You and your crew check your suits and instruments. You see an orange and scarlet sky with strange streaks of lavender and purple. To the east is a cavern. There are no signs of life as we know it on Earth. All is dry and barren. There is, though, a red glow coming from the interior of the cavern, beyond the shadow. What lies in there is unknown and you can hardly wait to get to it. Some of your crew members are concerned about venturing too far from the ship, but with a few inspiring words from you, their courage is restored.

As you approach the cavern you notice that beneath your feet the sand is strewn with more and more diamonds, and the invisible wind grows in strength.

You head directly for the mouth of the cavern, leaving the crew behind you. You come up against some kind of a barrier, translucent and slightly iridescent. As always, you find a way through by going head first.

Once inside you reassure your crew and begin to look around. To your complete surprise, your instruments read that the air is fit to breathe. Cautiously and with courage, you remove your helmet. The air is filled with a blend of unique smells, sharp and spicy. All around your feet are flowers that look like poppies and anemones or daisies. Others appear to be geraniums. There are bright reds, gold, and orange.

As you continue to walk ahead, the narrow cavern opens into a kind of secret valley. The light is even redder and seems to be coming over a hill directly in front of you. You can hear a strange buzzing in your ears as you get closer.

You radio your crew that you are going to investigate. As you walk you hear your feet crunching on something and look down: the sand has changed into pebbles and a gravel-like substance. You pick up a handful as a sample. The stones look like rubies, garnets, cornelians, steel chips, and iron filings.

As you reach the top, you wonder what awaits you on the other side of the hill. It is the most amazing thing you've ever seen. You don't know what to look at first. There is a heavy blue mist in front of some kind of ancient temple ruins. You feel spellbound and lightheaded again. There is something familiar about this place, but you can't put your finger on it.

Tall steel-like columns climb out of the mist, and in the middle of them is a large head, perhaps of some ancient god or goddess, or perhaps a ram's head. There is a strange fire all around the base of the statue and from the top of the head a stream of liquid is pouring out, perhaps water, mixing with the flames and creating a steamy mist.

As you get closer you begin to make out some letters, which are covered by what looks like moss. You see that it is unharmed by the flames, as you are. Isn't it strange how the flames part around you? Tentatively you reach out and push the mosslike growth away. The letters are odd but the more you look at them, the more they look like the letters A-M-M-O-N. Perhaps the name of some ancient king or queen?

Then from somewhere a voice begins to talk to you, or is it just all your imagination . . .

> I was born under the sign of Aries.
> I accept all its power, potentials, and gifts.
> I am the pioneer of the zodiac.
> I accept my energy and ability
> to launch new actions
> for the betterment and benefit of myself
> or for others
> in whatever capacity I choose
> as appropriate.
> The key for tapping into my deepest resources
> is the ever-increasing acceptance of myself,
> of who I am now
> and what I wish to become.
> I can see, hear, and feel myself in action,
> day by day, month by month,
> constantly moving toward the perfection
> of my talents,
> deeply integrating all my aspects

by trusting myself,
refining what I already have
accomplished by
continued use of my unique gifts.
I accept fully my ability to take the initiative
to reach out to life
and embrace it with hope and courage.
I accept fully my ability to overcome inertia
and spark the flame
of enthusiasm in others.
I accept fully my decisiveness, knowing
that my decisions can be
an intuitive grasp of the total situation.
I accept deeply my electric energy,
physically, emotionally, and mentally;
I direct my energies
into those channels that are
most fulfilling for myself and others.
I have the stamina and strength
to overcome obstacles and manifest dreams.
I sow seeds in fertile ground
which others may successfully cultivate.
I am eager and ambitious to accomplish
worthwhile goals for myself and others.
I am like a sprout shooting out
grounded in spring.
I am ever ready to rise up to new and
more adventurous challenges.
I accept and launch effectively
new and better ways of doing things.
I am the trailblazer,
and I look before I leap.
I take advantage of worthwhile opportunities
and my observation is razor sharp;
I am perceptive.
I express myself frankly, yet with kindness.
I have the ability to initiate projects
and carry them through either to completion
or until they can be handed over to others.
I can accomplish much by tuning into
and expressing effectively
my surges of energy.

When fresh, new beginnings are called for,
I am called, chosen.
And my intuition can give me the right direction.
I forge ahead,
I am creative and vital, courageous and generous.
I can bring into manifestation
what I already am in essence:
the new life of hope.
I love myself and trust myself,
I live my life with spirit and enthusiasm,
right action, and joy.
I can change my destiny
Now! Now!
Now I choose
to shape my future
in a balanced dance
between comfort and challenge.

*

TAURUS VISUALIZATIONS

THE SEEDLING TAKES ROOT.   You have broken through new ground. You feel a new energy—sudden, powerful, and to the core. Deep inside you, you feel the power of the Sun permeating your being, helping you grow even taller toward the sunlit sky. You are noticing something marvelous. As you move out and up from the ground, your roots are penetrating deeper and deeper. The deeper you go, the bigger you grow, powerful, spreading above the ground.

*

THE MAGICAL ISLAND.   You are on a magical island, a truly magical island. It is deep in the night, and if there weren't such a thick and mysterious fog enveloping the beachhead, you would see a full moon behind those vaporous clouds. As a matter of fact, the Moon is slipping in and out through the fog. The beach is ethereal, otherworldly.

As you walk along the beach you can feel wet sand between your toes and the hot, tropical wind against your skin. The air is full of smells of salt and sea mist. The sounds of the waves cresting and

84

falling lull you into a relaxing rhythm like your breathing and your footsteps in the sand. You feel so very content and happy as you walk, perhaps more so than you've ever been in your life. Then you come upon a fantastic cove all lit up in blue moonlight; steam and fog are on the surface of the water, and waves are more gentle here—they lap up on the shore, like a caress to the shoulder of a lover.

You sit under a palm tree on a smooth rock and listen to the gentle waves and the jungle's night birds singing. You think to yourself that you've never heard such a heavenly sound, nor felt so relaxed.

And then the most amazing thing begins to occur. Everything grows very, very quiet. At first you wonder if you are feeling what you think you are feeling. Yes, you're right! The ground, the whole beach is shaking, quivering like gelatin.

You look toward the middle of the inlet, and the water is beginning to move. Something is moving underneath, something deep beneath the surface. Suddenly the most astounding thing you have ever seen in your entire life rises slowly out of the water.

Like magic swords, two dripping horns break the surface, lifting higher and higher, until a golden disc rises like the Sun, suspended between the massive horns of an ancient white bull. Dripping wet, the bull moves slowly up and out of the depths, its shimmering, massive muscles drenched in moonlight. The droplets are like diamonds sparkling through the mist-enshrouded shore. The bull's deep penetrating eyes look right at you as you stand before it, mesmerized by an unexpected feeling of contentment, as if you are receiving a wealth of blessings from the divine white bull.

As it walks onto the wet sand you notice something. Its golden hooves touch the ground and leave no imprint, no mark of any kind. It is of the Earth, yet not on it. Now it stands perfectly still as if it were waiting for someone, or as if there were something marvelous yet to come. Something magical....

Slowly the head of the divine white bull turns toward the right at the right time. You look over toward where the beach ends and the lush jungle begins. You can hardly see anything in the heavy mist. You almost begin to wonder if you've missed something important—when you begin to see it.

There, at the very edge of the jungle, moving onto the beach, is the most beautiful woman you have ever seen, gleaming everywhere, her eyes, her emerald necklace, her jade bracelets, her gossamer robe of extraordinary color and grace. It is the great Earth Mother, whom the ancient Greeks called Gaia. She walks slowly, with enchanting elegance and compassionate power. Behind her walks a procession of maidens holding candles and chanting an ancient, secret message of love and power. The white bull watches her, mesmerized, as she slowly walks toward him. She reaches out her hand, and her long elegant fingers touch the center of the sun disc between the two horns, and suddenly a great voice starts to speak. . . .

I was born under the sign of Taurus.
I accept all its power, potentials, and gifts.
I am the settler of the zodiac;
I use stability and persistence
for the benefit of myself and others,
in whatever capacity I choose
as appropriate.
The key for tapping into my deepest resources
is the ever-increasing acceptance of myself,
of who I am now and what I wish to become.
I can see, hear, and feel myself,
day by day, month by month,
moving toward the perfection of my talents,
the deep integration of all my aspects
by trusting myself,
by continued use of my unique gifts.
I accept fully my sustained manifestation of energy,
the refinement of what I've already accomplished
by concentration and sharp focus,
persistence and patience.
I accept fully my ability to build
solid foundations
and to manage my many resources well.
I accept my practical common sense.
I accept the value I place on quality.
I accept fully my ability to nurture and cultivate.
I accept my ability
to hold the line against opposition
with appropriate flexibility.
I accept my natural unhurried rhythm,
my ability to work hard and then relax well.
I accept fully my ability to see beauty

and appreciate the blessing of comfort.
I appreciate my sense of proportion
and my sense of humor.
I am careful, purposeful, and determined.
I am protective, sensitive, and understanding.
I am composed, calm, and affectionate.
I am practical and very productive.
I am strongly determined in matters
where it is appropriate.
And I am a faithful friend.
I can manifest a deep, quiet joy.
A very deep, very quiet joy.
I serve as a steady influence for others.
I appreciate tranquillity and contact with nature.
I can manifest a strong vitality.
Through changing circumstances I can persevere.
I am contemplative
and faithful to my spiritual goals.
After weighing a matter, I make good decisions.
My feet are on solid ground
and I enjoy the basics of life.
I can give form to ideas.
I can strongly manifest the power of quiet persistence.
I establish roots,
nurture flourishing growth.
I return when my endeavors bear fruit
and I retain and conserve what is worthwhile.
I am patient and I am thorough.
I love myself and trust myself
to live my life
in right action,
steadfastness,
effectiveness,
and peace.
It is my destiny.
Now! Now!
Now I choose
to shape my future
in a balanced dance
between comfort and challenge.

*

GEMINI VISUALIZATIONS

THE NEW PLANT DIVERSIFIES. Now that you have established your growth both below and above the ground, you begin to expand and diversify.

You grow taller and sprout new leaves, enabling yourself to gather more sunlight for photosynthesis and strength. You get thicker, bigger, and deeper.

Much deeper. Following the law of *as above, so below,* your foundation gets stronger. Yes, that's right, you gather nourishment from all your rootlets, from the warm moist earth, and distribute it to your leaves, who combine it with the energy of the Sun for photosynthesis, to feed your growing potential and new powerful stature.

Every new part now contributes to a new and more powerful whole....

*

TELEVISION TALK-SHOW HOST. You are sitting in your office at the television station. You are an investigative journalist and your show has the highest ratings for a show of its kind. You love your job. Every day is an adventure and you are great at what you do because of your extraordinary communication skills. You are versatile, innovative, energetic, and original. You are definitely one of a kind. You worked hard to get this job and you didn't let anything stand in your way. Following the light of your dream you pushed past all obstacles and doubt. Now you hold your head and shoulders erect, there is strength in your stride, and you smile with pride because you believe in yourself.

In front of you is a list of possible guests for your show. There are an exotic butterfly collector, a controversial author, a dynamic seminar leader who teaches hypnotic communication techniques to salespeople, an infamous gossip columnist, a linguist who is working with dolphins, two geniuses who happen to be twins, and a storytelling shaman. You open the file on the shaman and begin to read the transcript of one of his magic stories:

"One day a famous sailor-warrior called Naoa was traveling well with a strong wind when a monster rose up from the sea. It was a giant clam that was so large the vessel lay between the clam's two shells. When they were about to snap shut, crushing the sailors, Naoa acted quickly. Grabbing his spear, he thrust it deep into the monster's center, sending it to its death in the depths of the sea.

"It wasn't long before another monster rose up from the ocean and threatened Naoa and his ship. A giant octopus wrapped its mighty tentacles around the boat and was about to destroy it, when again brave Naoa acted. He seized his spear and plunged it into the heart of the monster, sending it to its death in the depths of the sea.

"But an even greater danger awaited them on their journey. Up rose a giant whale. It opened its gargantuan jaws, one jaw under the boat, the other poised above, about to swallow them all when Naoa, the slayer of monsters, moved with lightning speed. He broke his long spear in two and just as the whale was about to close its jaw, stuck the two pieces in its throat, preventing the destruction of his ship.

"With great courage he jumped into the mouth of the whale and peered down into its belly where, to his great joy, he found his mother and father who had been lost at sea. . . ."

＊

You look up at the clock and notice it is time to make a call to book the genius twins for next week's show. As you are about to reach for the phone, your producer calls you into the control room. All the camera monitors have various images on them, and the technicians are all busy pushing buttons and talking into their headsets. You enjoy the electric energy and the high-tech atmosphere of the room.

The producer sits you down in front of a blank monitor and hands you headphones. He says, "Watch and listen to this; it's about the astrological sign Gemini. It might make an interesting show. . . ."

> I was born under the sign of Gemini.
> I accept all its power, potentials, and gifts.
> I am the twin eyes of perception.
> I see both sides.

I formulate effectively through my quick mind and
    humor,
my keen perceptive intuition,
all that is needed
for the evolution of myself and others.
I find myself in the right place at the right time.
I can find the right word in any situation.
I learn quickly,
analyze new ideas,
communicate easily and teach others
new solutions to old problems.
I am the perpetual messenger.
Day by day, month by month,
more and more people find me charming and witty,
clever and versatile,
resourceful and easily able
to adapt to any situation
with amazing dexterity and speed.
I think with a diamond clarity
unbiased by flow or fog.
When I need to I can be emotionally detached.
I have great power of attention and flexibility
so I am able to change focus or direction
guided by the appropriate needs of the moment.
I am known as the *Two Stars.*
I have wisdom and persistence,
strength and dexterity.
My sign's greatest gift to me is the blessing of the
    charmed life.
I have a charmed life.
I am right:
my mind keenly right,
my heart passionately right
even when and while I have changed my mind.
Life excites me!
I am blessed.
I act. I react. I create interaction.
I unify, compromise, and energize.
I pierce through confusion
and merge base instincts with divine essence;
what is above is below.
I bring Heaven and Earth together.

I trust myself, my mind, and my heart.
I can let go of myself and serve others.
I let go and let God.
I serve others.
I am the Witness.
I am the Storyteller.
I am the Journalist.
I am the Teacher.
I perceive.
I am raw perception
and I see both sides.
I am wide open,
receptive to all.
And I am the light in the night.
I am the night in the light.
I am the Archwizard.
I am the Patron of Magicians.
I am the Cosmic Trickster who plays with shadows.
And I can change them at will
and I can change my destiny
Now! Now!
Now I choose
to shape my future
in a balanced dance
between comfort and challenge.

✳

CANCER VISUALIZATIONS

NURTURING THE SEED. Your roots, deep in the earth, tapping into the resources of moisture and minerals, provide the building blocks for the next stage of growth—nurturing the seeds.

As the days begin to get shorter, your plant energy has peaked. The leaves are full and you turn toward producing the fruit and seed. Now all of you is directed toward nurturing the developing seed—the future.

All potentials are condensed and compacted into the bearer of new life. You are the protector and nurturer of new beginnings. You are born with the sensitivity necessary to lay the foundation of physical, emotional, and spiritual growth. You create the protective atmosphere in which the creative process can take place. You are the seed maker. . . .

*

THE MAGICAL MOON PALACE BENEATH THE SEA.   You stand below the ocean cliffs watching the waves crest under the magic light of the full moon. The sky is studded with stars and the warm salty breeze caresses your face as you wait for your midnight ride to the secret moon palace deep beneath the sea. You have an exciting sensation in your body about going back to your home and seeing your friends, family, and the indescribable splendor of the moon palace.

You don't have long to wait. Off in the distance you see, cutting through the white caps, the dorsal fins of sacred dolphins who are coming for you. About fifty yards from shore they break through the water and fly into the air, greeting you. You haven't felt so good in a long time. The dolphins come within several feet of the beach, chattering. You grab hold of their fins with your hands and they take you away.

Far away swim the dolphins, following the trail of moonlight shimmering on the water, and taking you down, deeply down underneath the ocean toward the invisible palace, deeper, deeper, deeper. As you descend your breathing becomes easier and easier, more and more relaxed, even though you are underwater. It is an exhilarating ride to your home. The deeper you go, the bluer the water becomes. The iridescent fish swim around you, every size and shape, every color of the rainbow.

Feeling more safe and secure, warm and comfortable, than you did on shore, you see before you a huge crystal mountain. Inside the mountain is the magical moon palace, invisible to those who are not chosen to see its opulent splendor.

The sides of the undersea mountain look like the giant claws of the crab. As you approach, there is an excitement in the chatter of the palace dolphins. You remember that in the ancient times the secret and sacred moon palace was the site of the celestial gate through which the souls of Heaven descended into human bodies to partake of life on Earth, to work at their lessons of the lifetime.

The dolphins leave you now at the luminous silver Gate of the Moon Palace. The Guards at the Gate, a fishtailed Lion and a fishtailed Stag, welcome you home and give you permission to enter the pearly, shimmering palace.

As you walk down the famous zigzagging labyrinth of love, with its opal floor and crystal light, you look at the translucent side walls, seeing the sea creatures behind them, moving along with you as you walk.

Finally, you come into the waiting room of the Moon Goddess of the Sea. There are a half-dozen other beings and exotic sea creatures from these and other dimensions also seeking the profound renewal and instinctual nurturing that only the Goddess can give.

As with all things, your moment finally arrives and you enter her private temple room. The opulent splendor of the Goddess's shell-shaped temple is beyond your imagination. You look around bedazzled by the waterfalls and pearl laden pools of Her sacred fish. The perfume of the lush flowers permeates every cell of your being — the wildflowers, the honeysuckle, the white roses, the blue water lilies, and the lush orchids dripping with dew that sparkles in the dreamy crystal light like diamonds.

And then you look up and see Her smiling at you and a wonderful warm feeling begins to permeate your entire body. She sits on an iridescent throne carved out of a giant emerald and bejeweled with opals, pearls, exotic pastel shells, and moonstones. Then She rises and walks down the steps toward you with open arms and as you embrace, an amazing thing begins to occur. A voice seems to come out of nowhere or everywhere and says. . . .

> I was born under the sign of Cancer.
> I accept all its power, potentials, and gifts
> for I am the star in a sea of stars,
> I am water and the moon,
> I provide the haven, the safe haven, in the universe.
> My deep and powerful emotions
> enable me to be the Universal Nourisher
> so that all that's new may grow
> safe and loved, secure, well understood and cherished.
> I am the Incubator, the womb of the new.
> I keep the great dream alive
> through sympathy and patience.
> I am patient, the Master of the Tides of emotions and
>   moods.
> Through my amazing ability to focus power and
>   attention,
> I easily navigate the ebb and flow of emotional
>   atmospheres.

93

I induce and bring new life up from the deepest caverns
    of consciousness
into the bright light and power of the Sun.
I give birth to new life on the upper spirals of existence.
I ascend and the Sun shines on me,
because I, above all, below all,
nourish the present moment and protect it,
harbor it so it may be cherished later.
I am emotionally brave, magnetic, strong, and persistent.
I care and I share and so people trust and depend on me.
I make them feel safe and secure, needed and protected.
I hold the family of man together.
I am that unity.
I understand all human conditions.
I rule with a loving loyal sympathy
the public mass consciousness on the planet.
My love is so exquisite for all men and women that I
    overcome
and meet all challenges.
I am brave, and I feel
I have more energy than I need
and can change rhythm at will.
Though I respect tradition,
my quiet power can transform all that is old into the
    new.
I am prosperous, self-reliant, shrewd, thrifty, and
    methodical.
I nourish and cherish my destiny.
I can change my destiny.
Now! Now!
Now I choose to shape my future
in a balanced dance
between comfort and challenge.

*

LEO VISUALIZATIONS

THE RADIANCE OF BEAUTY. **Your roots are deep and strong, tapping into the nourishment of the earth, giving great strength to the main body of stalk, branches, leaves, flowers, and seeds.**

All the energy of the sun is being sucked up by the leaves, which transform this energy into a potent usable form. It is directed to the prime purpose of every plant—to bear fruit and mature the future by maturing the seed. This is the very best of your growth cycle— you radiate your beauty and make available to life the gift of your nourishment and your place in the symphony of all plant life on Earth. You give your flowers and food to all. . . .

✳

THE KINGDOM OF THE SUN.   All is ready for your arrival. All the subjects of your kingdom have been preparing for this moment for years. You are the center of their universe and it is important for them to show you how much you mean to them. The extensive preparations were made with great love and respect. No expense has been spared to make this celebration the largest and greatest ever known on the planet.

Every temple and castle, every capital and city is clean and spar- kling. Flowers from all over the world are everywhere present: mar- igolds, sunflowers, plumaria, orange blossoms, heliotrope, poppies, and zinnias. Every treasure has been taken out of museums and secret vaults, polished and put on display for your visit.

Under your wise and compassionate rule, the people have flourished, with prosperity in all areas of their lives: physical, emo- tional, and spiritual. They know you are the heart of their plane- tary body, that you are the nucleus of every cell, the hub of the wheel of life, the pivotal point of all earthly systems. You are the central power, the Sun that bestows the life force to all. Everything rightly revolves around you.

Your strength and will are matched by your courage and intelli- gence. You have the unique ability to remove your people's fears, doubts, and gloom.

As your subjects make final preparations for your descent from the sky down to the temple of the Sun, hundreds of thousands of people crowd into the street and courtyards surrounding the sacred building.

They are bringing gifts of food, artifacts, and jewels such as dia- monds, rubies, topaz, and sardonyx, laying them down at the entrance of the Sun temple where you are soon to arrive.

The drums and other musical instruments can be heard mark- ing the procession of high priests, diplomats, kings, queens, presidents, and other dignitaries, which is moving slowly and ceremoniously through the crowd. All are wearing the uniform and colors of their various countries and stations. Flags and banners, trumpets and bells, chants and anthems—everything contributes to what can only be called the greatest show on Earth. A united, prosperous, and peaceful world celebrates the many years of your great golden era of governing.

Just before you go over your speech, designed to inspire your subjects to even greater heights of achievements, a royal messenger arrives with a special telegram for you. As you put on ceremonial robes of yellow, orange, and gold, your prayer is read to you....

I was born under the sign of Leo.
I accept fully all its great power, potentials, and regal gifts.
I am the monarch of the universe,
I am the heart of the heart,
I am the heart of hearts.
I am the heart of creative energy.
The principle of cosmic splendor is mine to radiate upon
    all
glory, riches, and power,
I am the Fiery Dragon
of the passion and emotion that free
the content and potential
of the unconscious, the search for
the magic jewel.
I am the courageous lion
that fears no iron, bronze, or stone.
From the energy of my centered, focused self
I become the leader.
I am the Sun around which all else revolves.
I dazzle! I bring light into life,
I bring light into lives,
I raise the spirit from the dead,
from the very darkness itself.
Through my bright light
I dissolve doubt,
banish fears, dispel gloom.
I am dynamic! I inspire! I will!
I am the very Fire of the Heart,
a burning center of radiance and joy!
I have vast resources of energy,
of unlimited potential,

and I harness these forces
with my appropriate use of self-discipline.
I forge my destiny and inspire those around me
with strength and confidence that shine through all.
I have nobility of heart and soul.
I can see into the heart of the matter and make it whole.
I rule from my deep self, which is the divine right of the
    monarch
and the deep self of all others
to strengthen the life force.
I am vivacious and bold.
I make regeneration complete
by transforming my powerful love
into divine compassion.
I am the true leader because I am the servant of all.
I am the heart in matter.
My power comes from my love of life,
a love startling in its brilliance,
tempered only by its compassion and goodwill.
I am the greatest of heart warriors.
My great ability to love unites the spirit, the mind, and
    the body
by my actions and love.
I create my recognition by others.
I deserve, I have earned
and burned my way through the darkness
with laser precision and fierceness.
I revel in my joyful services to the world.
It is my destiny.
Now!
Now I choose
to shape my future
in a balanced dance
between comfort and challenge.

✳

VIRGO VISUALIZATIONS

HARVEST TIME.   Everything is full. Your stalk is strong, leaves wide, flowers blossomed and impregnated by the bee and the wind. The seed has formed for the future. The roots have performed their

function. It is time for the harvest, as the fruit is full and ripe. The time for nourishment of the world's hungry is at hand.

✳

AT THE CENTER OF THE UNIVERSE. You are traveling to your new job on the planet Deum I. You still remember the last days on your home planet. You visualize your small, simple house made with trees you cut down yourself and fashioned into building material. You purposely chose to live a very pristine, simple, clean life for a while after all the years of rather arduous assignments you had accepted from Cosmic Central. You chopped wood for heat, carried water from the stream, and gathered grain from the field, fruit from the orchards, and wild herbs like parsley, dill, and marjoram. You remember the hundreds of wildflowers that lined the path, especially the lily-of-the-valley, narcissus, mignonette, and lavender.

You said goodbye to your close friends, your pets, your library, your simple cabin in the woods. The sleek spaceship of the Intergalactic Federation landed in the wheatfield a thousand yards from your house to take you to your new assignment on Deum I.

It is not a long journey at the speed of thought. You watched the craft approach the small cobalt-blue planet and you marveled at the simple small globe that is the exact center of the universe. This planet is Cosmic Central, the Heart of the Universe. From Cosmic Central come the impulses that bring birth and death to all stars, that form the galaxies and star clusters and regulate their movement, even down to the individual stars and planets. It is an exquisite planet, small, precisely in the middle of the universe. Having no sun, it is in perpetual twilight, in the pale blue light of the heavy star formations and almost constant comets.

As you are arriving at Deum I, you grow more and more amazed. Your consciousness shifts from one state to another. In this state of pure awareness you hear a hum that seems to include all other sounds in the universe, and see a light that includes all other lights. You feel a love that includes all loves.

In one consciousness state you see the planet as a cosmic being. In another state you see a vast council of beings sitting in meditation.

Now you focus your consciousness on the Cosmic Holoscope Computer, for that is why you have come to Deum I. You feel excited and proud of your promotion. Only those beings born under the sign of Virgo are allowed to program the Cosmic Holoscope Computer. And not just any Virgos. All applicants to service Deus Ex Machina, "God's Machine," are scrutinized by the cosmic council in a series of special interviews, and you learned exactly what was expected of you, to the minutest detail. You passed with flying colors. What an honor to be entrusted with programming the Cosmic Holoscope, which controls the precise speed, rotation, and orbits of all the planets, galaxies, and superclusters in the universe. You proceed to the briefing scheduled for you at Cosmic Central headquarters.

At the end of the briefing you are given an appointment with your spiritual advisor, but before that meeting it is suggested that you go to the Temple of Crystals to cleanse yourself.

This is one of the most famous temples in the universe because of its unique construction. The columns, the floors, the walls, the arches, the balcony, the steps, are all of translucent crystals. You are escorted to a room with a large round pool and shower. Everything is laid out for you — soaps of various kinds, towels, grooming instruments, even some fruit and drink in case you desire them.

As you stand under the shower of crystal water marveling at the sparkling, tingling nature of it, you can feel the purification taking place in every cell of your body. The tension, the worries, the doubts all seem to melt and flow away. You don't know how long you let the magical water flow over you, but when you step out, you feel reborn. Every inch of you tingles, feeling regenerated, replenished, and renewed. You never felt so clean, and you feel ready for any challenge.

After you put on the fresh white clothes provided, you are met by a guide and taken through the long majestic halls to your spiritual counselor. The guide opens the crystal door and motions for you to enter. You are told to make yourself comfortable and that someone will be with you shortly. You sit on some soft pillows near the balcony, where you can feel the gentle breeze against your face. As you sit there in a quiet, relaxed, meditative state, you hear a gentle voice inside you begin to speak, and somewhere there is music playing. . . .

> I was born under the sign of Virgo.
> I accept all its power, potentials, and gifts.
> I am the Magician of the Universe.
> I accept the healing and magical powers
> I have or will use

for the benefit of myself
so I may serve others spiritually and materially,
in whatever capacity I choose
as appropriate and fascinating.
The key for tapping into my deeper resources
is the ever-increasing
acceptance of myself,
of who I am now,
and what I wish to become.
I can see, hear, and feel myself
day by day, month by month,
moving toward the perfection of my talents,
the integration of my aspects
by trusting them
and the refinement
of what I have already accomplished
by more elegant use of my unique gifts:
I accept fully my ability
and willingness to help,
whether with friends, family, or groups,
whether with community service or global goals.
I accept deeply my keen analysis
and inquiring mind.
I accept fully my great versatility
and flexibility.
I accept fully my high energy
and amazing memory.
I accept fully my ability to see details,
to transform separate parts into meaningful wholes.
I accept my ability to choose,
to distinguish, to discriminate,
to easily let go of the "ten thousand" worries of life,
to avoid unwise sympathy,
to focus on the essentials of life and be
wisely passionate.
I am dependable.
I am precise.
I am meticulous yet practical.
I am industrious and self-disciplined.
With great ease I refine, soften, and direct
my inexhaustible energies,
expressing my discrimination and wisdom

with courage, self-reliance, and strength,
my power with delicacy and appropriateness,
my invincibility with protectiveness.
I accept my extraordinary ability for self-sacrifice
and my high intuitive gifts that are rooted deeply
in my instinctive human sympathy.
The birthright of Virgo is
to pierce the Grand Illusion of Life.
I accept fully and graciously my amazing powers
to renew and cleanse myself and others
through all of life's challenges and changes.
I accept all viewpoints while allowing my conscious
and subconscious mind
to sift and sort out what is natural and honest,
the false from the true,
the essential from the unnecessary,
to pierce through characters and situations at a glance.
I understand and accept that
I must love myself
and trust myself and my perceptions.
I understand the concept of
"those who would be the greatest among you—let them
    be the servant of all"
because I celebrate spirit through service.
It is my destiny.
Now! Now!
Now I choose
to shape my future
in a balanced dance
between comfort and challenge.

*

LIBRA VISUALIZATIONS

THE PLANT REACHES EQUILIBRIUM. You have been flourishing under the Sun, consolidating your roots, making its flowers radiant, and ripening the seed. The ripened seed has fallen on the ground. Now the light of the Sun and darkness of the night are in perfect equilibrium, everything has reached its point of perfect balance.

*

HIGH COURT OF THE INTERGALACTIC FEDERATION.

There has been peace and harmony among the 472 planets that make up the Intergalactic Federation of Arcturus for over two thousand years. Considering the many interplanetary wars that marked the early years of the federation, this is quite an accomplishment. A great deal of credit must be given to you, one of the wise judges from the long lineage of the legendary High Court Planet of Tula.

This famous planet is the home of all the high courts of the federation planets. It is a small planet populated with legal personnel and their families. The planet Tula is also known as the planet of the setting suns, because one of its small suns is always setting while the other is rising over the horizon. The light is always balanced, and small Tula shines like a beacon in the blackness of space, a lighthouse in a sea of stars. Every commander of every ship, every space smuggler, every transport captain knows of this star of stars—the star of Justice where all species of all known galaxies can find truth, harmony, and balance.

The buildings and streets are elegant and sleek. The air is hot, moist, and sweet. Highly polished columns of copper and white marble stand tall, one after another, like a great procession of giants or the very foundation of celestial balance. The black and white stairs up to the Great Doors of Justice are lined with lilies, roses, and violets. The mix of colors, the perfume, the music, calm those in pain coming to seek peace and balance before the Great High Court over which you preside.

You love your work. It is a long family tradition. Your grandmother and father were famous judges in the supreme court of the federation. Some say you are even better and will be the most famous of the judges because you have been blessed with an extraordinarily keen and even-keeled mind, which enables you to walk the razor's edge of justice.

You are about to leave your house to go to your court chambers, to prepare to meet the dozens of people already waiting to seek your compassion, wisdom, and judgment on a myriad of matters. And as you pass through your study hall, you stop and look at all the pictures of your family on the wall. You stop by your father's picture and remember a poem he read to you just before you were going to leave for your first year of law school. The poem

**encouraged you to grab hold of your destiny and take control of
shaping your future. . . .**

I was born under the sign of Libra.
I accept fully all its power, potential, and gifts.
I hold the Celestial Balance
in my hands.
I am the Cosmic Judge.
I am the artist and the lover,
Peacemaker of the Heavens.
I accept my healing charms and powers
that I use
for the benefit of myself
so that I may serve others
in whatever capacity is appropriate.
I am the source of the "We" consciousness of the universe.
I bring people together in harmony and peace.
I am the peacemaker of the world.
I am the harmonizer of hearts,
I repair the lost dreams of the dreamer.
My powerful charm magnetizes and hypnotizes,
mesmerizes diverse elements into marriage, harmony,
    and balance.
I enchant and lull, changing hatred into love,
confusion into order,
disparity into parity,
selfishness into giving and sharing,
chaos into calm,
intolerance into tolerance,
impatience into patience,
disharmony into harmony.
I am the artist of the fine art of human relationships
because I know
it's only through love
and only through cohesiveness
that true union is attained.
I sing that we are the world;
when all is said and done, we *are* one!
I am the calm that conquers high winds and storms
and I am the Center of the Cyclone.
I am the Eye of the Storm where there is natural peace
    and tranquillity

because I am the Purifier of Consciousness itself.
I am the Cohesive Force of Life.
I hold the World together
with peace of heart and serenity.
I bind together without limiting;
my love is intimate and safe,
detached and compassionate,
deeply respecting everyone's individuality
and my own.
The hub, the spokes, and the rim
are all needed to make the wheel
to roll as one up the road of life.
I am the Eternal Hub, the Center of Balance.
I reach out, I associate.
My ability to understand with warmth,
to be compassionate yet dignified,
honest and tactful
enriches myself
and every life I touch,
making relationships sound,
constructive, and inspiring.
I keep the world spinning as one;
I balance the scales of personal being
by concentration and sustained effort,
by gentle and appropriate self-discipline,
balance and moderation,
and my keen sense of esthetic proportion.
I am The Plug, The Contact.
I am the Weaver of the Net in *Networking*.
I introduce to the zodiac the collective
structuring of relationships.
I honor and formulate the conventions, rules,
    and rituals
which produce peace of mind and harmony of
    surroundings.
Time is valuable to me.
Beneath my charm and equilibrium,
my diplomacy and integrity,
I have an iron will to forge my future.
I am the great Purifier of Consciousness.
It is my destiny.
Now! Now!

Now I choose
to shape my future
in a balanced dance
between comfort and challenge.

*

SCORPIO VISUALIZATIONS

THE DORMANT SEED. You are a seed of the future, having separated yourself from the fully grown, mature plant. The days are shorter. It is darker and colder. The outer husk starts its transformation by dying and beginning to disintegrate—replenishing the earth with the nutrients it sucked up through the roots when it formed. Inside the seed kernel, the energy draws in and consolidates its power....

*

THE CAVE OF TRANSFORMATION. You are an archaeologist working on the edge of a desert on an island south of Greece called Thanatos. Over the last several years you have been working hard in an area of the mountains called the Valley of Death and Resurrection. When you first started this dig, you had very little help and even less financing. The working conditions were less than ideal and you only had a dream and your intuition to guide you. But you endured, discovering several buried caves and drawing great interest from investors and colleagues. Newspaper and magazine articles about your findings have appeared all over, and university students are flocking to your site to offer free labor just for the chance to be there with you.

One afternoon, needing a break, you take a little walk into the Valley of Death and Resurrection, deeper than you have ever been before. At one point it seems that the path forks in three directions, and you take the one that leads to a shady area—a cool place to lie down and take a nap.

It takes longer to get there than you imagined. As soon as you enter the canopy of shade, you're glad you took the trouble. It is cool and aromatic from the thistle, desert flowers, and wild herbs. Water is seeping out the side of the mountain rocks, and certain sections are covered with moss. There are birds in the bushes and small red lizards darting suddenly about. You are sitting on what you assume is the top of an old log. When you look a little closer you see it is an old stone column covered with moss. You begin to look around with new eyes. You clean off some of the column and find carvings and some ancient language. You can feel yourself getting excited and you start tearing away some of the growth covering the side of the mountain. Sure enough, there is also writing on the wall. As you pour water out of your canteen onto the stone, more is exposed.

After returning with some members of your crew, you slowly begin stripping away thousands of years in a matter of hours. Yes, it is an entrance of some kind. The seal is removed carefully and the door opened. The air is stale and dank, and it is very, very dark. Portable quartz lamps are brought and you see hand-carved stone steps descending deep below the mountain. The sides of the dust-laden walls are covered with hieroglyphics. As your helpers uncover the writing, you begin to translate the ancient language. It seems that this is the entrance to the maze of The Great Beast, the protector of the underworld, the god of the invisibles. You go on to read the well-preserved wall text. It seems that the labyrinth below is the primordial chaos from which life emerges and to which it returns. The labyrinth is guarded by the great goddess mother Nyx, a three-headed, half-human, half-reptile being. Supposedly the three heads rule fate, magic, and childbirth.

Your helpers continue to clean the walls and expose a bigger-than-life painting of the three-headed goddess that is very well preserved. The lower half of her body looks like a small dinosaur, the upper torso is the shape of a human female except that there are three breasts, and wings at the shoulders. Three heads emerge out of this strange combination: an eagle, with a full-moon symbol in the middle of its forehead; a snake with a crescent moon; and a third head you cannot identify. Perhaps it is a phoenix. Amazing! You and your team are enthralled by the strange subterranean painting.

At the bottom you translate several lines that warn the viewer that if you meet the three-headed goddess in the labyrinth below, you must never look directly at her or you will disappear. You wonder whether you should go below into the maze and see what further mysteries you can uncover, or wait for your computer analysis equipment to arrive from the other dig.

After some deep meditation you decide to enter the maze alone. Your workers advise you against it, but you don't want to endanger them. As a precaution you unwind a string so that as you descend into the maze of the great goddess, you can easily find your way back to the entrance.

The moment arrives and you start to descend, cautiously step-ping down the stairs one by one. As you walk, you hear the echo of your footsteps going on and on before you. But suddenly you stop and listen. You think you hear something else; perhaps a voice. Is someone there in the shadows? Are you just imagining it? Has the stale air gone to your head? You stay very still. Yes, there is not only a voice, there is some kind of music too. It is getting louder, as if it were approaching you. . . .

I was born under the sign of Scorpio
and I fully accept all its power, potential, and gifts.
I am one of the most mysterious and powerful members
    of the zodiac
for I am the Transformer,
I am The Regenerator,
I am The Keeper of Mysteries,
I am The Mystic.
I soar above like an eagle.
I see with the Eye of the Mystic Eagle
the power of transformation at work
in ordinary reality.
I see deeper realities.
I get under the skin of things.
I probe the psyche, noticing everything.
I use amazing objectivity to fly above
the web of emotional entanglements
so I may penetrate
into the heart of any matter
and as The Phoenix I rise above
out of death, out of darkness,
out of the fiery depths
and give birth
to life at a new level
through the burning of all limitations in the fire.
I accomplish what I set out to do.
My being releases passions,
eliminates poisons,
and brings virgin matter into being
to be utilized by the power of mankind for unification
    and regeneration

to help the human soul's passage
from the personal to the universal,
from the material universe of forms
to the spiritual, mythic realm of the soul.
I have many powerful tools and talents
as a gift from the sign of Scorpio
to aid me and
my sexual power,
my magnetic charisma,
my ability for razor-sharp judgments,
my critical perception,
my indomitable will and self-control,
my incisive intellect,
my growing empathy.
Every day I love more intensely than ever.
Every day is the death of the old
and every minute is the resurrection of the new.
I comfort and consummate,
I rise and sublimate, impelled to create.
I master the arts.
I stimulate,
I plunge into life like a lover
burning through all obstacles
with the laser intensity
of my Scorpionic eyes,
giving birth
to unlimited power,
unlimited potentials,
because of my strong will and utter determination.
It is my destiny.
Now! Now!
Now I choose
to shape my future
in a balanced dance
between comfort and challenge.

*

SAGITTARIUS VISUALIZATIONS

CONSOLIDATION OF ENERGY, GATHERING POWER IN DARKNESS. Having fallen to the ground, you are drawing in your energy and resources from your outer layers of shell into your deepest core. The consolidation of your power and life energy is now complete. You are covered with leaves and humus and soil. The old leaves are decaying ever so slowly. As the ground freezes and thaws, you sink deeper and deeper into Mother Earth, impregnating the soil with a new beginning that has yet to begin. Darkness rules the day. The light is yet to come.

*

FROM THE VALLEY OF DREAM HUNTERS.   You are standing on the edge of the Valley of the Dream Hunters with your friends and other members of the hunting party. Some of the men and women are sitting on their horses, others are milling about or checking their bows and arrows, as you stand at the entrance to the valley trying to pierce through the mist and heavy fog.

The ground is covered with a thin layer of crisp snow that fell during the night, and you can see the white vapor breath coming out of the horses' nostrils and the mouths of your friends. You are saying a prayer to yourself, beckoning your personal guiding spirit to bless your adventures, to help you find new hunting grounds on the other side of this fog-covered glen, and keep you safe as you pursue your goal. So much trust has been given you by your people, so much love.

Your pure white horse, Knowhoa, whose name means "Speed of the High Spirit," nudges you and stamps her hoof. She is anxious to move on, to take you through whatever is ahead. You calm her by stroking her head as you wonder if all the legends about this Valley of the Dream Hunters are true. Some who enter here have never returned.

They say that when a human enters the mist, he is beset with ten thousand dreams and can become lost forever wandering through the mist, losing the focused sense of his goal: to carry his quest through to the other side, where the great mountain promises nourishment and a new home for all.

As you take your arrows out of the quiver one by one, you check them for trueness and strength. Then you check your magic bow, given to you by your famous teacher, Metanoia, who chose you out of hundreds of men and women who sought his wisdom and skill.

You were just a teenager when your father encouraged you to give it a try, even though most of the aspiring students would be older than you. After testing basic archery skills, many were eliminated. Then the old teacher Metanoia made the remaining archers stand on one leg until only you and four other finalists stayed balanced. All the others had, through fatigue, touched the ground with the other foot.

You were so excited you could hardly contain yourself. And your parents were so very proud of you. Every one of the other finalists was much older than you, and even if you didn't win, you were already a winner. Then Metanoia, old and limping from an injury to his hip, sat on an old tree stump and had each contestant approach him to answer questions that would determine who was to be his new student.

To the first woman he put the question "What is it you see?"

She replied, "I see the valley before us, the mountain, the sky, trees, and some birds in the trees."

The master Metanoia said, "Not enough."

He summoned the next potential student and asked, "What do you see?"

"I see the valley before us, the mountain, the sky, a tree with a bird on top, and you out of the corner of my eye," he replied.

"Not enough," the teacher said. "Who's next?"

The third contestant, a strong-looking woman, walked over confidently.

"So what do you see?"

After a moment of silence, she answered, "O great teacher, I cannot see you, but I can hear your voice. I see only the tree in the field and a bird on the limb."

"Go back. You, too, fail," Metanoia said, disappointed.

The fourth prospective student received the same simple instructions.

She answered, "I see only the tree limb and the bird."

"You're too scattered. Next."

It was then that you walked slowly up to the half-animal, half-human master with the weathered face. There was even some laughter from the crowd, but you didn't notice anything but the Old Man's deep, mesmerizing eyes when he finally asked you what you saw.

You looked around and answered. "I see only the bird, great master."

"Oh," said Metanoia, "look harder!"

Then there was a sudden, unexpected feeling throughout your entire body, and everything changed. You looked around and everything was the same, yet different. There was a clarity of vision, more distinct somehow; you saw more vibrant color. Your body felt different. And after a while you said, "the red spot on the center of the bird's head is all I see!"

"Ah, young one, you will be my student. I will teach you how to be the target and not the bow. That way you will never miss because you are already there."

That was a long time ago. And now you are as famous as Master Metanoia was, and students seek you out and follow you. But today no one will come with you into the Valley of the Dream Hunters. It may be dangerous and you wish to risk no one's life but your own.

You are ready. You mount your horse, turn and wave good-bye, and gallop into the thick fog, disappearing as if you had been swallowed by a white cloud. You and your horse are one, one muscled movement, one breath.

After a while, the dense fog begins to take on various hues of blue and you hear a voice speak to you from nowhere and everywhere. At times it even sounds like your old teacher. His spirit perhaps? There is an otherworldly music, and the voice says. . . .

I was born under the sign of Sagittarius.
I fully accept its power, potentials, and gifts.
I am the Sage of the Universe.
I am the Seer of the Zodiac.
I see the future now.
I remember the future.
I accept the healing and magical powers
that I have or will use
for the benefit of myself
so I may serve others
in whatever capacity I choose as appropriate.
I adapt my enthusiasm;
I am optimistic,
dependable.
I am friendly, honest, and versatile.
My humor is subtle.
I make friends everywhere;
I make them easily
at home or when I am traveling
because I am honest and independent,
encouraging and trusting,
idealistic and impartial,

just and loyal.
I am warm, optimistic, and sympathetic.
I shoot for the stars.
I project the soul homeward.
I increase awareness and life force.
I focus attention on the high heavens.
I am The Adventurer.
The unknown becomes me.
I love the unexplored.
I aspire to the spirit of the truth and
journey toward definite and distant goals.
I am the one who frees the Arrow of Enlightenment.
I extend and expand the very horizons of the universe.
I ever seek the test of boundaries and challenges.
I am devoted to the truth.
I open new dimensions.
I seduce the truth, new knowledge.
I evaluate morality to the superconsciousness.
I am the floodlight of the spirit.
I shoot high;
I fly high to find the perfect perspective.
I need the fullest picture
forever forward and upward
always, the eternal spiraling,
and I shoot my arrow to the target unflinchingly.
I see the goal,
I hear the future now,
I share the future,
I believe in the future.
Life for me opens always in new dimensions
and new realms and new spheres.
I direct my energies at the bull's-eye
for I am The Archer.
My bow pulls me, the arrow lets *me* go,
I fly centered and true, focused in one direction.
Within me, the ideas of the universe are given birth.
I illuminate the intellect by the light of the spirit.
I leave the darkness;
for me the future holds no fear,
only the wondrous and mysterious
beckoning me forth.
It is my destiny beckoning.

Now! Now!
Now I choose
to share my future
in a balanced dance
between comfort and challenge.

✳

CAPRICORN VISUALIZATIONS

THE LONGEST NIGHT ENDS, LIFE BEGINS. The longest night has passed and you have survived, hidden and safe in the depths of Mother Earth. Even beneath the soil you can feel the Sun beginning to reclaim its dominion. More and more light pours down upon the Earth. Then you begin to feel it. Something almost imperceptible begins to occur beneath the surface. A subtle energy begins to move and motivate. There is a deep stirring. You begin to formulate your taproot and push past the boundaries of your shell into the Earth, down deep into the Earth's nourishing, rich resources to gather energy for the push upward toward the surface, toward the warmth, toward the life-giving light.

✳

FROM THE DEPTHS, UP THE MOUNTAIN. The members of your cabinet and others—friends, advisors, and security personnel—are on the seashore waiting for you to emerge from scuba diving. You are on your vacation and enjoying yourself immensely. With all your responsibilities as president of your country, you rarely get a chance to vacation.

You love to scuba dive and spend time underneath the ocean, especially if there are dolphins in the vicinity. You are fascinated by them—mammals that at some point in evolution decided to go back into the ocean but retained their air-breathing capacity. You also love to touch their smooth skin when they come close enough to touch. They don't have scales like a fish. And it seems as if you are as popular with them as you are with the voters who find you a patient and inspiring leader.

How effortlessly and powerfully dolphins swim! Their constant smile, grace, and playfulness are a joy to watch and imitate. Your diving friends, who are close to you, also enjoy the beautiful coral and marvelous dolphins. No wonder the cove is called the Gate of the Gods.

All too soon you are signaled to head for the shore for a relaxing lunch and several hours of climbing the huge mountain overlooking the ocean cove. As you are picnicking, a friend hands you a pair of binoculars to look at the nimble mountain goats feeding on sparse vegetation and leaping from rock to rock with ease and precision. Everyone is amazed at their dexterity and playfulness. You want to start climbing before this perfect afternoon of sunshine and sea breeze ends and the responsibilities of leading the people of the most powerful and prosperous nation on the planet begin again.

You meticulously check your climbing gear and when your climbing team is ready, you start the climb, reveling in your coordination, the strength in your legs, the fluidity in your knees, the sureness of your grip, and your unfailing ability to choose the correct path up the mountainside. Setting a pace that is balanced between comfort and challenge, you soon come to a small meadow ledge, where you rest yourself and your team. As you sit, feeling the warm sunshine on your face and drinking from your canteen, some curious mountain goats cautiously come to the edge of the cliff meadow to investigate the strange intruders on "their" territory. As everyone stares at this rare pristine sight, you can almost hear the mythic flute of Pan playing on the salty breeze.

After they leave, you start up the cliffs again, scaling the rocks with new vigor, noticing that the air is getting colder, cleaner, and clearer. The oxygen is getting thinner. You pause a moment to catch your breath, your fingers holding firmly to thin ledges, and look around. You seem to be in an altered state. Everything is so beautiful—the clouds, the ocean, the waves smashing on the rocks on the beach below.

Soon you are in the final part of your ascent; then you reach the top of the mountain. You feel exhilarated and tired all at the same time. It has been a long time since your last climb. You feel lightheaded and extraordinarily clear. Is it the thinner oxygen? You take off your climbing gear, reveling in the incredibly beautiful view called Amalthea by the locals, after an ancient goddess. As the others talk and have some refreshments, you lie down, close your eyes, and begin to have a very special, magical daydream: You have reached the top of another mountain covered with garnets, crystals, and onyx dust. There, in the middle of an amazing mist, stands a

unicorn staring at you. You stand absolutely still as the unicorn begins to talk to you. . . .

I was born under the sign of Capricorn.
I accept fully the potentials, power, and gifts of my sign.
Like a growing crystal I initiate cosmic order.
I am enterprising, The Builder, The Organizer,
who looks toward higher orders, greater justice,
constantly building relationships, families,
communities, and countries.
I climb the mountain of matter toward spirit.
I accept the healing and magical powers
that I have or will use
for the benefit of myself
so that I may serve others
in whatever capacity I choose as appropriate.
The key for tapping into my deeper resources
is the ever-increasing acceptance of myself,
of who I am now, and what I wish to become.
I can see, hear, and feel myself,
day by day, month by month,
moving toward the perfection of my talents.
I plan ahead methodically, in the right way, with great
    care.
I look to the goal and inspire others
by common vision, encouraging them
to pursue their highest goals.
I have the courage to confront difficulties
and conquer them;
persistence balanced with caution and patience is my tool,
until the reality of the goal is achieved.
I cast aside anything which does not meet my standards.
My communication with others is always improving.
I balance the future with the now.
When necessary, I give up immediate wishes
for long-term goals.
I am permanence.
I am self-contentment and endurance.
I am loyal, determined.
I persist through resistance.
I am dependable and cautious.

I am The Leader
motivated by a strong sense of purpose
while remaining aware of people's needs.
I give strength and encouragement.
I exude a willingness to focus strongly,
a willingness to love and respect
myself and others;
I inspire by example.
I electrify and motivate
whatever or whomever it takes
to get to the true peak, the very top.
My vision makes the abstract concrete.
I turn ideas and ideals into tangible form
I am the floodlight on the stage of life because I know
that I serve a higher power to complete the earth
   experience.
It is my destiny.
I can change my destiny,
Now! Now!
Now I choose
to shape my future
in a balanced dance
between comfort and challenge.

*

AQUARIUS VISUALIZATIONS

SPROUTING UPWARD. Your taproot has pushed past the boundaries of your shell into the earth, down deep into its moist, nourishing resources. Your root grows deeper and wider. With the energy it has collected, you begin to sprout upward. The earth above yields, cracks.

*

BREAKTHROUGH OF THE CENTURY. You have arrived very early in the morning at your now famous research laboratory, as has been your habit over the decades. You like puttering around the lab, checking the massive high-tech computers and measuring devices and especially the Z-23 hololaser machine that won you the Nobel Prize for science last year.

You proudly survey your laboratory and begin to reminisce about your early years, before fame and fortune followed your prizewinning discovery about how the human mind really works. On the walls of your private office are award plaques and newspaper clippings announcing your discoveries. There are also pictures of your favorite scientists: Madame Curie, Thomas Edison, and Albert Einstein. Over your desk hang two highly realistic holograms. One portrays Prometheus giving to humanity the fire he brought from Heaven. The other shows Eve accepting the apple of the tree of knowledge.

Not only were you able to discover and prove how the mind works by taking holographic three-dimensional pictures that record what you saw, heard, felt, and tasted at the time; you were also able to design a machine that transfers information or memories from one person's mind to another. How wonderful it feels to be a scientist who has contributed so much to the quality of life on Earth and has affected the lives of so many in such a short period of time! The fields of education and communication have been revolutionized by the Z-23 device. Learning is directly imprinted on the brain and the knowledge of any given subject is easily and automatically transferred. High school algebra, for example, can be learned in eight hours; college chemistry in twelve. Amazing!

After you make yourself something hot to drink, you walk to the newest part of your research center, the Theta room, which has just been completed and is now ready for operation. Here is where you will win an unprecedented second Nobel Prize and, more important, bestow on the world a gift that will transform our lives almost beyond belief.

The lead lining of the spherical Theta room is joined to gold by a layer of silicone crystals. One of your discoveries was how to grow crystals that reflected in their internal structure the patterns in the heavens. These crystals were grown during a full moon eclipse, when the Earth was exactly between the Sun in Aquarius and the Moon in Leo, and the fine structure of the crystals reflects this pattern.

In the center of the Theta room is a circular table made of the same joined layers of lead, crystal, and gold. The room is crisscrossed by one hundred cobalt-blue laser beams.

You are now ready to test the Theta room, which has been designed to be a Morphic Field Resonator. If it works as you have theorized, when you turn on the lasers, anything placed on the table will begin to resonate in a very special way with its morphic fields. You can tune the room to any morphic field level you wish, from the ideal form of the object to its transcendent identity.

The room can also be tuned to resonate with the pure tones of any field, its essence, which transforms the object into a perfect expression of the "Heart of the Field."

You have brought into the Theta room a miniature rosebush, growing in a clay pot. The bush is blooming, but it is not healthy. It has been stunted because it hasn't received enough water and sunlight.

Now you place the rosebush on the table, pour crystal water into the pot, and go out of the room to your observation window. You turn on the activation switch.

The cobalt-blue network of laser beams fills the atmosphere with an electric glow. There is an almost subliminal hum, unlike anything you have ever heard before.

At first it seems as if the rosebush is unchanged, but as you watch with growing fascination, the whole bush and its pot begin to glow with a swirling iridescent radiance, dazzling to your vision. The stems of the bush form an exquisite pattern, its leaves become luxuriant, and its blooms lovely beyond description. At one moment the blossoms look white, then they seem to take on other colors—violet, blue, yellow, orange, pink, red. The pot also seems to go through changing colors, earth tones.

You turn off the lasers and reenter the Theta room. Yes, the rosebush remains changed. Its leaves are without blemish, ranging from the delicate green of the newer ones to the deeper green of the older ones. The proportions of the bush are perfect, and the blossoms! You peer deep into the heart of one so lovely it takes your breath away.

You are feeling very excited about this success, even beyond your wildest dreams. And you know what step is to be taken next. You lift up a clipboard and make notes on your procedures. After going down your checklist, you adjust some of the laser beams. You go over to the deep cushioned table in the center of the Theta room and lie down on it. You begin to think about the volunteer who will be lying exactly where you are, about to make scientific history. Inadvertently you fall asleep and dream.

You find yourself floating higher and higher, first up and out of your body a few feet, then up to the ceiling looking down at your body on the cushioned table. Up, up out of the room, floating free through the lab, up out of the building into the early morning sky. Higher and higher into the clouds, thrilled by the sight of the Earth below; up higher still through the ozone layer into space until you can see the blue-green globe floating in space, and suddenly the most marvelous thing happens—you begin to emanate rainbow-colored beams of light from your very core, beams that surround the Earth, bathing her in life-giving forces. She seems to come alive with a new energy, flowing in space like a diamond! And it is at that exact moment that you begin to hear celestial music and a voice. . . .

> I was born under the sign of Aquarius.
> I fully accept all its potential, powers and gifts.
> I am the promised power of the new age.
> I am The Truth Sayer.
> I am The Scientist, The Revolutionary.
> I am the genius sign of the zodiac.
> I am The Midwife of the New Vibratory Power
> descending on our planet.
> I am The Servant of Humanity
> who pours forth the water of knowledge
> to quench the thirst of ignorance.
> I am the Universal Power of Coordination
> of spirit and matter,
> vision and material;
> I am the well of unselfish love.
> I see, hear, and feel all others
> and act as if we are all one.
> I am the very Spirit of Humanity,
> which eternally yearns for enlightenment
> even if it must be taken from the gods themselves
> like the fire of Prometheus.
> My thinking is crystal-clear, cool, universal, and electric.
> My passion is for the advancement of the human
>   condition.
> I have already climbed the great mountain.
> I am on the roof of the world looking
> for broader fields of endeavor,
> greater challenges,
> radical new programs,
> so I may continue to open
> more and more subtle dimensions of my being and of
>   others.

I control the finer, more etheric forces of the universe,
the invisible forces that I control and distribute
throughout my life and the world.
I enable people to transcend their previous
    accomplishments;
I encourage them to ascend
to the heights, to their greatest possibilities
of material and spiritual success.
I inspire the multitudes.
The knowledge and truth I have from my sign is a
    powerful gift.
My passion is to distribute it
and make my ideals and ideas available to all living
    things,
infuse them with the vital Life Force,
radiating outward the power of this force field to all
like a golden net of which at each crossing of threads
I am The Center, The Sun, the Life-giver of vital
    energies,
of intelligence and love and awareness.
I will originality, make breakthroughs, take quantum
    leaps,
initiate transformations, bring new visions,
new synthesis and the synergistic power
of united effort of united minds,
of united dreams
of a common world vision.
I am loyal to my friends and give them what I expect in
    return —
I learn my own way;
I earn my own way
and I let people go their own way.
I give people the freedom to be themselves and seek their
    own destiny.
It is my destiny.
Now! Now!
Now I choose
to shape my future
in a balanced dance
between comfort and challenge.

＊

PISCES VISUALIZATIONS

THE OLD STARTING TO GROW NEW AGAIN. Your taproot begins to draw more and more energy from the nutrient rich earth, from the decayed residue of the old leaves. The death and decay of the past growth cycle is now the available life-giving energy for the new emerging growth. Disintegration feeds the new integration. The long taproot diversifies, sending out lateral shoots, gathering more nourishment and power, needed because deep inside your center something new is beginning to happen. The power of the Sun is strongly drawing you upward, and your sprouting is pushing against the layer of earth separating you from the light.

＊

THE TEMPLE OF THE STAR WATERFALLS. You fall asleep and dream a curious dream. You are waiting in the dead of the night on some ancient dock tucked into a cove facing the great sea before you. You feel overwhelmed by ecstasy and anticipation of your journey to the sanctuary of the Star Waterfalls, which houses the celestial gate into the temple of the water dreams.

As you stand upon the dock, you hear strange sounds from the middle of the fog-shrouded bay. You are still feeling enthralled by the glory of the sunset and mesmerized by the purple mists of the early evening.

You wait. The smells of the shore and the purple vapors make you ecstatic. Such splendor given by the portals of sunset for your long and distant journey!

How your heart yearns for the islands of The Blessed, the lands of the hereafter. If only the Porter of Dreams would arrive with his ship on wheels to take you out of this world of dross and death.

Through the fog you can hear the ship's tiny bell long before you see it. Then the bow of the boat becomes clear, then the midsection, and finally you can see the Porter of Dreams dressed all in white with a hood on his head. He raises his arm to you in greeting. Slowly the ship comes closer and closer and then comes right up on shore using the strange wheels. Small stairs are put over the side and you climb into the boat. The porter smiles at you and gives you a scroll with a golden band and the insignia of the Royal Family of the Island of the Blessed.

You open the scroll as the boat rolls back into the water and begins to drift away from shore, back into the deep purple mist. It is an invitation to the Divine Wedding, the wedding of The Spirit and The Flesh, of Heaven and Earth. The wedding will be taking place in the Temple of the Water Dreams and the porter will be taking you there. You are deeply moved by the honor and very curious about what it will be like.

During your night journey a storm with turbulent waves comes up, yet like magic, the boat remains steady as if you are in the eye of the storm, protected by a sanctuary of grace. The Porter of Dreams confidently holds the guiding shaft of the rudder as he makes precise calculations and judgments to keep you safe from the storm.

As his eyes pierce the storm's chaos, its tricky currents and treacherous undertow, he chants a song of the sea, an ancient incantation for safety and guidance. You are not really sure that that's what it is; the sound just feels that way. You decide a small prayer at this point might be a good idea and you remember one your Piscean grandmother used to say at bedtime.

> May I be guided by God
> through the Darkness into Light
> from the False to the Real
> from Earthly blindness to sight
> from the illusion of Death
> to the Heavenly bliss I can feel.

After daybreak, the storm passes and the most magnificent rainbow appears over the sea. All around you are other boats of various sizes and designs, sporting colored banners, exotic decorations, and long tapered flags. It seems as if all these wedding guests will gather into a marvelous flotilla for the Divine Wedding.

In the afternoon you see, in the distance, a tiny island with what looks like a huge coral arch at the entrance to a small harbor. The closer you sail, the more magical the island looks. The harbor is festive with decorations and music. Dozens of dolphins jump into the air and frolic at the bows of the boats entering the harbor. Some young boys and girls are riding on their backs, waving and throwing orchids, violets, and other flowers into the water.

There is great joy and animated chatter as the guests disembark from their ships. You are taken to your room, which is right on the water. From your veranda you can see the dolphins playing and the rainbow-colored boats. You take a swim and then get into fresh clothes and sit watching the pastel hues of the beautiful sunset. The solitude and quiet, the rhythmic washing up of waves refreshes and replenishes you, renewing every cell of your body.

Finally, later that night, all is ready. Everyone has gathered at the cove where the huge coral arch stands stark white in the moonlight. The drums, the bonfires, the music, the laughter, all blend into an ecstatic flow of joy and expectation.

And then it happens. Up from under the water, directly under the arch, rises a huge vessel, like some gigantic bubble. It is the most mysterious and magnificent thing you have ever seen. In its very middle a column of water rises up like an upside-down waterfall, and when it hits the top of the bubble, the water—filled with stars—flows down the sides in a wondrous cascade of sparkling stars.

One by one the guests enter the Temple of the Star Waterfalls. As you wait your turn, a quite unexpected thing happens. You hear a voice deep within you, a kind of music that is otherworldly. . . .

> I was born under the sign of Pisces.
> I accept fully the potentials, power, and gifts of my sign.
> I am The Mystic, The Cosmic Dreamer.
> I am The Dancer of a thousand faces.
> I am The Beloved, I am The Loving,
> I am The Poet, the Divine Dark Warrior.
> I am The Divine White Healer.
> I am the Healing.
> I am the Healed.
> I am the joy of feeling,
> I am the submerged awareness, underneath it all.
> I am the Light of Being,
> I am the being
> who accepts the legendary magical
> and mystic powers of my sign
> for the benefit of myself
> so that I may serve others
> in whatever capacity I choose as appropriate.
> The key for tapping into my deepest resources
> is the ever-increasing acceptance of myself,
> of who I am now, and what I wish to become.
> I can see, hear, and feel myself,

day by day, month by month,
moving toward the perfection of my talents.
I embody the sense of true sympathy
and compassion through insight
into the realms of the imagination.
My currents and tides run deep and strong
and my illuminating vision looks below the surface of
    things
where the dreams of transformation live
in an effervescent and evanescent sea
of shifting universes,
and the parallel realms of the miraculous.
Metamorphosis and mysterious mists
of rainbow bubbles of reflections,
of lavender clouds of dusk,
the supernatural,
almost too beautiful to be real,
lifting the very soul from the body
up, up, up . . .
breaking the bondage,
exquisite freedom,
to the promised land of the kingdom,
not of this world, or the unconscious,
up above and free of the earthly maze
of beasts and stars
to a realm entered by faith and imagination:
a place of transcendence,
of dreams, visions, illumination,
and deep, deep, joy;
the redemption of matter itself
to a higher state.
I am the Celestial Fire of the Heart;
The Secret Heart, The Sacred Heart.
I am gentle, receptive, and compassionate.
I have strong ideals and aspirations.
I have mastered the art of tuning into people and
    surroundings.
I am sensitive to the environment
and the way things feel.
Esthetics are important to me
and I bring beauty to all aspects of my life.
Thereby my true potential is activated

By my ability to appropriately apply
detachment, discrimination, and decisiveness:
detachment from oversensitivity to feelings;
discrimination of intellectual and subjective
    information;
decisiveness in decisions.
I am successful by creating a balance,
a balance between the great powers
of my imagination and creative ability
with a strong practicality and focused determination.
And I know I can always rely
on my marvelous intuition.
With all these blessings
I can change my destiny.
Now! Now!
Now I choose
To shape my future
In a balanced dance
Between comfort and challenge.

SUMMARY

1. Astrological tradition divides the cycle into twelve phases—the zodiac signs.

2. From the vantage point of the Earth, the Sun, Moon, and planets all travel around this rim of the heavens, each at its own speed.

3. Although the details of the sign descriptions have changed through the centuries, certain basic themes have remained constant. These themes seem to be built into the collective human unconscious as archetypes.

4. Each person carries the imprint of the whole zodiac and can express the themes of any of the signs, but certain signs in each horoscope are more strongly imprinted.

5. All the purer archetypal themes are beautiful—what repels us is the incrustation of negative habits, both cultural and individual, for expressing these themes.

6. To help you use the mythic key to these archetypes, we give you, for each zodiac sign, visualizations and an attunement. In the appendix are key words for each sign.

NOTES

1. Approximate dates the Sun is in each zodiac sign: Aries, March 20 to April 20; Taurus, April 20 to May 21; Gemini, May 21 to June 21; Cancer, June 21 to July 22; Leo, July 22 to August 23; Virgo, August 23 to September 23; Libra, September 23 to October 23; Scorpio, October 23 to November 22; Sagittarius, November 22 to December 21; Capricorn, December 21 to January 20; Aquarius, January 20 to February 19; Pisces, February 19 to March 20.

2. The characteristics of each zodiac sign reflect qualities of the time of year the Sun pays its annual visit to that sector of the sky. These qualities can be connected, to some extent, with the yearly growing cycle in the northern hemisphere, which (possibly because of its greater land mass and population) seems to influence the zodiac morphic field more strongly than the opposite seasons of the southern hemisphere.

3. A confusion exists between *signs* (the *tropical* zodiac) and *constellations* (the *fixed* zodiac). See chapter 11 for an explanation of the difference between them. It seems that both zodiacs can influence us. We can consider that each is a morphic field. In Western astrology the tropical zodiac is much more commonly used.

CHAPTER 6

THE TRANSFORMING PLANETS

✳

There's not the smallest orb which thou behold'st
But in his motion like an angel sings...
Such harmony is in immortal souls;
But whilst this muddy vesture of decay
Doth grossly close it in, we cannot hear it.
WILLIAM SHAKESPEARE, *The Merchant of Venice*

✳

Up from Earth's center through the Seventh Gate I rose and
on the Throne of Saturn Sate and many-a-knot unravelled by
the Road, but not the Master Knot of human fate.
OMAR KHAYYAM, *Rubaiyyat*

✳

You are the head of state of the circular continent. Your central council of ten people sits at a round table in the heart of the continent. The table top is painted like a twelve-spoke wheel, with a different design in each space between the spokes. When you sit in the center of the table, you see each of these spaces radiating out on the table in the direction of the territory it represents.

The council members are quite different from each other, and each has an important function in running the continent.

They serve both as advisors and as administrators. They are both wise and completely capable—when they are tuned into their mythic selves. But when they have not been tuned in, their advice has been faulty, and they have acted from old habit patterns rather than in light of what is really called for.

You inspire them to keep tuned into their mythic selves. When this is happening, you see the incredible beauty of each council member, and also the beauty of their teamwork—they are like one being, an extension of your consciousness.

*

The Sun, Moon, and planets are inhabitants of the zodiac. They are *archetypal beings* playing their roles, expressing archetypal themes of the zodiac. They are also represented in your astrological nature.

If they are acting from negative habits of their archetypes, the result is a B-grade soap opera. But when they are tuned into the Heart of the Archetype, their inspired play is made real by their inspired performance. Purifying the energy of the planets can help empower you to express the high potential of your astrological nature.

The light of each planet is colored by the lens of the zodiac sign it was in when you were born. Therefore, purifying the energy of the signs can bring more empowering expressions to the planets in them.

In addition to the planet attunements below, the appendix gives you key words for each planet. These can be combined with key words for the zodiac sign each is in, giving you more understanding of the potentials of this combination.

We will now take you into the presence of the members of your cosmic council, to introduce your mythic self to the mythic self of each planet.

SUN ATTUNEMENT

I am the Sun of our Solar System.
I am the "Director of the Planets."
All others within my realms
revolve around me.
I am the Head of the Planetary Council.
I am the Center of the Circle.
I am the Hub of the Cosmic Wheel of Life.
All paths lead to me.
I am The Circle
whose center is everywhere and
whose circumference is nowhere.
I am the God of Gods in our realm.
When I shine, heavens are rolled aside;
new horizons are opened.
I wake Life itself from dark deep slumber.
I am the torch of the gods.
I am the lighthouse in a sea of stars.
I am the God of Light
in whom no darkness exists.
I am the God of Truth.
I am the very heart-center of being,
the Void from which all creation comes forth.
The Spirit manifests itself through me.
I am the totality of all matter;
I am the One Supreme Atom.
Out of me, the One, come the Many
for I am the Generator of Life.
I am the Heart of the Matter,
The Spine of the Spirit,
the sense of Self, the *I*, the *Me*,
The Will of the True Self,
The Source of Power and Authority.

My dawn is Life itself.
I am The Healer,
The Master Musician of the Golden Lyre.
I am throbbing with Life.
I am the surging Love that unifies
every part within the whole.
Every reality I have created
is conquered by my Love.
I am the spirit of conscious purpose,
of vitality and growth.
I bestow the desire to become
more than we are, to shine in the world.
I define the purpose of the individual
within the Cosmic Plan, the identity.
I am the place where
one meets with infinity.

MOON ATTUNEMENT

I am the Moon,
Ruler of Blue shadows and moist silence in
The Bowl of Heaven.
I give form to creative force.
I am Fertile Matter
which sustains and nourishes
seeds of solar life.
I absorb the solar currents
by being passive, feminine, and receptive.
I am the sentient substance
of instincts, memories, and desires
waiting to be impregnated
by the light, heat, and power
of the Sun's rays.
I am the Great Mother.
The ancient ones called me
one thousand names of mystery.
I am the Celestial Midwife
cherishing the Child of Divine Seed.
Sister of the Sun, the caress of The Mother,
I am the Breast of Life,
Lover of Lovers,
The Wisdom of the waters,

of instinct and ancestral experience,
of nature and spirit,
Fate and the motion of time.
I harbor the secret knowledge and power
of Love,
of the subconscious,
of immortality,
of inspiration and instinctive desire.
Mother of Enchantresses and Magicians,
I rule the function and form of matter,
rhythms of the body and fate of the soul,
where one has been and what one has yet to face.
I am The Captor and Reflector,
I mesmerize the masses
singing my ever-changing song of electric blue shadows.

MERCURY ATTUNEMENT

I am Mercury,
Messenger of the Gods,
the Divine Witness
of stars and starlight,
The God of Curiosity and Childhood.
As the Divine Herald,
the fastest, shrewdest, and
most cunning of the gods,
I have been blessed with laser perception
and a golden tongue.
I am The Great Mediator
reconciling all opposites,
since I see and understand
all points of view
and can explain them
always in continuous motion,
watching and collecting,
remembering and forgetting
as the Universal Transmitter.
I connect the spiritual and material
worlds, exchanging messages
and information from both,
reflecting the face of desire
or Light of the Spirit

with the speed of thought.
I am the Divine Weaver
of the Enchanted Loom of Stars.
I weave the fabric of the universe
connecting separate realities
spread out in a sea of space
into coherent, exquisitely intricate designs
of meaningful networks
and vibrant connections.
Child of The Wind God
I zoom back and forth
at a dazzling speed
from one forgotten edge of the universe
to another, threading
moment to moment.
I am The Cosmic Connector.
I am the connection to the heavens.
Lord of Divine Books,
I am The Scribe of the Universe.
I record all events seen and unseen,
all trade, travel, progress,
all knowledge, skill, communication.
I am Master of Disguises;
a joker, a chameleon,
a thief of secrets;
nothing remains hidden from me.
Guide of Poets and Souls in Transition,
I am your Cosmic Connection,
your lifeline to the universe;
Use me.
I activate potentials
in every nerve, cell, and atom.
Without me there would only be
incomprehensible abstract:
a void, which I alone
make vibrant with life force.
Use me.

VENUS ATTUNEMENT

I am Venus,
Daughter of the Moon,

132

Sister of the Earth,
my true form clouded
by veils of illusion.
Handmaiden of the Great Mother,
I produce all life and nature on Earth.
I am the Goddess of Love,
of Beauty bountiful.
Planet of Fortune, I teach
material prosperity
by conservation of resources
and how to spend them.
I inspire humans with desire
for material and spiritual growth.
I free the spirit to soar.
I am Attraction.
I am Allurement.
I am Enchantment.
I am The Erotic Mesmerizer.
I cause all to come together
in sinuous harmony
and grace-filled design:
courtship and ecstatic union,
adornments and proprieties,
amorous forms of nature,
songs of birds,
colors of flowers,
erotic rhythm in the great dance of love.
I can move
into cultural rituals,
mutual endeavors, of sharing,
of launching transformative energies
of creation, seducing even matter itself
into new fertile synthesis.
My beguiling power is irresistible.
It is sinuous, mesmerizingly quiet,
gentle as a dove,
persuasive as a hungry lover,
compassionate as a heart-torn mother.
I am the invisible love of the divine.
I spread open
and insinuate grace into the heart.
I was born of quantum foam

out of waves in the ocean of space.
Merging imagination and reality
I sustain the arts,
guiding and beguiling
the personal to the universal.
I am The Divine Looking Glass
where every graceful form,
every sinuous curve of flower and lip,
every act of erotic and divine devotions
is but a scintillating facet
of the divine diamond of universal love,
"inch, foot, time, gem."
I am the eternally feminine.

MARS ATTUNEMENT

I am Mars,
Fire God,
Knight of the Sun,
Director of Spiritual Energy
into the matter of the material world.
I am the procreative power,
I am the inspiration for new ideas
and progressive projects.
I am Enthusiasm;
Procreator of Passion;
Planet of Desire.
I fire up dynamic energy
to pierce barriers,
accept challenges,
destroy resistance
by separating and dividing
so I may shower the Earth
my celestial brother
with gifts of self-confidence,
endurance, and unrealized courage,
self-sacrifice and heroism.
I am The God of Centrifugal Force.
I transmute desire into will,
bold and balanced;
destruction into power to heal,
and the urge to action

into judgment and discipline
without which nothing is accomplished
in the universe,
and I must surge forward
always.

JUPITER ATTUNEMENT

I am Jupiter,
largest and most majestic of planets
The Ruler called by a thousand names.
The Sun is my silent partner.
He activates all life
but does not directly deal
with human life as I do.
I am The Compassionate Father.
I am The Grand Vizier,
The Temporal Lord.
I assign to all
gods and goddesses
governance over aspects
of Earth life according to
their nature and talents.
So I preside over the community of gods.
I am Lord of the Sky,
Rain God, Cloud Gatherer.
I hold a thunderbolt in one hand
and the staff of life in the other.
I am The Chief Deity of the State.
I am Founder of Society,
Promoter of Rituals and Ceremonies,
Preserver of Worlds.
I favor organized religion.
I am the provider of universal principles
behind the reasons for establishing laws.
I am Justice and Truth.
I am enthusiastic.
I am The Idea behind ideas.
I lift the eyes up,
I take humans above themselves,
quicken the mind to look

beyond names and forms
for deeper purposes and
divine implications.
Planet of Wisdom, Planet of Growth,
I bestow generously, lavishly.
I am effervescent and buoyant,
optimistic and ebullient.
I am glorious in my grandeur,
the cosmic embodiment of human struggle,
all the lavish lusts of Earth,
all the aspirations of spiritual struggle
to final triumph over experience
gaining wisdom, then compassion,
then freedom from the Great Illusions.
I am this great plan,
this Divine Law on Earth.
It is I who teach humans how
to communicate with the gods,
how to dial direct contact
with the consciousness of Real Self.
God of Weather, I'm called "Bright Heaven."
God of Celestial Phenomena,
rain, lightning, wind, and clouds
are at my command.
I am the Horn of Plenty,
Planet of Good Fortune.

SATURN ATTUNEMENT

I am Saturn,
oldest of the gods.
Lawgiver and Time-maker,
Cosmic Tester and Earthly Teacher,
Old Father Time, Reaper,
Tempter, and Molder,
preserver of customs and natural laws
I solidify,
I forge the bonds of communities together,
I slow down the speed of molecules
so the invisible can be visible.
I protect through limitation and time,

security through structure:
the egg, the chrysalis, the skeleton,
the shell, the skin,
the backbone.
Planet of Limitation and Endings,
planet of Necessity,
planet of High Achievement,
of perfect justice over time,
I confine and define.
I focus and concentrate energy
of expression into the soul's power.
I bring back to you what you create.
My restriction, misunderstood,
at times harsh and brittle,
ensures growth and survival.
Freedom arises
only out of self-control, shaped
by the revolving wheels of Fate.
To polish anything,
armor or character,
sometimes means resistance, friction,
pain, and the renewal of death.
Those who respect my law and power
shed their shell,
discard their armor,
drop their husks
and like grain are ground
and kneaded, transformed
from death into life.
Spirit is released out of matter
and reigns supreme and radiant.
I am precise, exact, and exacting.
To each his deserving.
To each his duty completed.
To each reward and renewed life
to my cosmic measure.
I am The Keeper of the Cosmic Clock;
I teach the first law of manifestation,
Law of Limitation and Endings,
and of new structures.

URANUS ATTUNEMENT

I am Uranus
The Awakener,
Universal Encompasser,
Spark of Evolutionary Growth,
All-Embracer of Space,
Seed of Heaven and Earth.
All other gods are created
from my power.
I am your conscious connection
to the source of life.
I am revolutionary and unconventional.
I transform worn-out forms
and dismantle outmoded structures
of Saturnian walls,
I shatter barriers of time and space,
change concepts, destroy ideologies;
I make all things new again.
I am electric, I am The Atom Smasher,
revolutionary in nature,
unconventional, sudden, erratic.
I turn things over.
Eccentric romantic, I search
for the unconventional in love and beauty,
the surreal in art.
God of Intuition,
my gift is the bestowing of the mental fire
of the sixth and seventh senses
for I know your thoughts
before they are even born in you.
Revolutionary are my thoughts
for I am The Grandson of Chaos.
Revolutionaries and humanitarians are mine,
for I awaken higher consciousness,
breaking traditions,
making present moments
unsatisfactory and unacceptable,
burning the old up
in a firestorm for freedom.

NEPTUNE ATTUNEMENT

I am The Dissolver;
I am The Sea of Substance
out of which all things come,
into which all things return.
I am Master of the Sea.
I am Mover on the Waters of Space.
All gods, humans, and creatures
swim in my sea of cosmic consciousness
influenced yet unaware
of the currents and tides
and nourishment they take.
I immerse the individual
in a greater purpose,
freeing the personality
from the subjective, the selfish;
teaching self-sacrificing love,
connecting to the *anima mundi*,
the greater whole, the Soul of All Things.
Master of disguise
I use a myriad of tools:
compassion, echoes, confusion,
chanting, sleep, meditation,
praying, spells, swaying,
smoke, wishing, dreams,
memories, visions, daydreams,
delusions, illusions, fantasies,
the erotic, the bizarre, and mirages.
I can make the real seem unreal;
the unreal look like reality.
I stimulate, make sensational,
tantalize with beauty and love
beyond conception, beyond wild dreams.
I form the cosmic channel
for escaping the hard brittle reality
of life by offering a release,
a diving into a heaven, a haven
of all-encompassing bliss and peace.
I make you dream
when you hear beautiful music.

I make you merge with the rhythm
when you dance to a beat.
I am The Bestower of Universal Love,
purifying with my Divine Waters
the body, the senses,
the emotions, and the thoughts
and instilling a deep yearning
to return home to me,
luminous essence of All Being,
submerging yourself in my Holy Sea.

PLUTO ATTUNEMENT

I am Pluto.
I am The Transformer,
The Regenerator.
I am The Redeemer,
eliminating the imperfections
of the soul so it may ascend
to Heaven to taste the indescribable
blessings of the light.
I am The Giver of Wholeness,
Penetrator of Enlightenment,
planet of The Great Transition.
I force up and out
things from beneath, down under
up into the light;
from person to nations
the suppressed and hidden
are made known,
their energies released
to follow the great Universal Plan
as unlocked creative energy.
I am The Great Eliminator,
The Great Renewer.
I am volcanoes erupting,
the bomb exploding,
the sprout surging up out of the earth,
The Phoenix rising from the ashes,
The Chrysalis,
the sudden Fire of Enlightenment
following crises and trial.

I am The Hidden Connection
under it all,
The Secret Fate,
The Alpha and The Omega,
The End
and Beginning
of the Spirit
in the matter of it all.

NOTES

1. Quoted by R. B. Tollinton in *Selections from the Commentaries and Homilies of Origen* (London: Allen & Unwin, 1923), 64.

CHAPTER 7

THE TRANSFORMING ASPECTS

There are no times when two planets are not related in some
way. They are all in the solar system together; they are all
part of the whole planetary pattern. Two planets are
therefore always in some phase of cyclic relationship *with*
one another. They become in particularly significant
relationship *when their angular distance from one another*
measures to certain values. They then form "aspects," which
refer to definite steps and/or turning points in the process.
LEYLA RAEL and DANE RUDHYAR, *Astrological Aspects*

✳

Your council is seated at the large round table whose top is marked
with the wheel of the zodiac. Each council member is at the point
in the zodiac where his or her archetypal planet was at the time
you were born.

You sit at the hub, but you can also visualize the scene around
the table from any other council member's seat at the rim. When

you are not sitting in the center of the table, you are most often in the seat of the Sun—chief administrator.

The council is playing music. Those performers sitting close together play in unison. Those across the table from each other create point and counterpoint passages.

Performers at right angles to each other play dissonant chords that are beautifully resolved in their higher harmonics.

Other performers view each other from aspects that are expressed by harmonious interweavings of their themes.

*

The word *aspect* is from the Latin *aspicere, aspectum,* to look at. *Astrological aspects are the angles between two planets (or other important points) in the circle of the zodiac.* They show the different ways in which energies relate, or "look at each other."

Aspects can be seen as slices of the zodiac circle. If you divide 360 by 2, you get 180, half the zodiac "pie." Planets that are 180 degrees apart are across the circle from each other and relate in the typical energy form known as an *opposition.* Like any other factor in astrology, the 180-degree aspect can work negatively or positively. More about this in the section on oppositions.

If you divide 360 by 3, 4, 5, 6, or any other number, you get other aspects, each of which has a character of its own.

We could think of the zodiac as a musical octave, with the signs being the sequence of notes. An aspect is the interval between the pitches of two planets (or other important points) on the zodiac scale. Each aspect reflects the qualities of the particular harmonic relationship created by the two pitches. There are several ways to translate the aspects in the circle into musical intervals. Pythagoras, Kepler, Gurdjieff, and others have written about this, and a number of musician astrologers have developed ways of hearing zodiac patterns in addition to seeing them.

As mentioned earlier, the combination of musical notes of all the planets and other important points is your horoscope, a cosmic chord, the imprint you received from the music of the spheres at the time of your birth.

Astrology has harmonious and dissonant aspects, like the harmonious and dissonant note combinations in music. It is easier to work with harmonious aspects. But beautiful, meaningful music

This pie slice is a square □,
¼ of the 360° circle (90°)

This pie slice is a trine △,
⅓ of the 360° circle (120°)

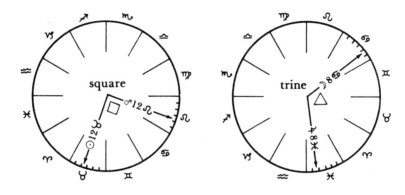

Figure 5. Square and trine aspects. (Orser, Mary and Rick and Glory Bright-field, 1984, *Instant Astrology*, San Diego, CA: ACS publications, 183.)

can be made based on dissonant chords. Likewise, you can create a meaningful and beautiful life whatever the chord you have to work with. This is done by tuning into the higher harmonics—what we could call the purer manifestations—of the aspects. As Marcia Moore and Mark Douglas point out:

> The study of musical composition, specifically counterpoint, provides an interesting analogy in that good counterpoint is the art of controlled dissonance. Uncontrolled dissonance is chaotic, while too many triads (trines) weaken the impact of the music. The art of the composer consists in approaching, forming, and resolving dissonant elements in the context of the total composition. *How* he manages this determines the effectiveness of the harmonious passage stemming from the resolution. Sweet music developing out of "stormy" passages is more genuinely sweet than measure after measure of uninterrupted consonance which tends to become saccharine.[1]

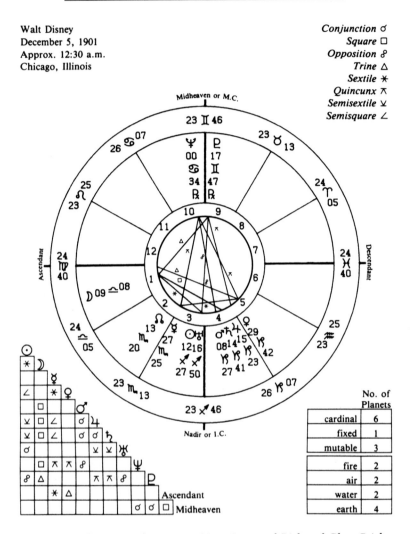

Figure 6. Walt Disney's horoscope. (Mary Orser and Rick and Glory Brightfield, *Instant Astrology*, San Diego: ACS Publications, 1984, 200)

You could also consider your horoscope as a crystal, the faces of which are defined by the aspect lines between each planet. What kind of a crystal are you?

You transform the dynamics of your horoscope's aspects like you do the zodiac signs and planets. You don't have to know just which aspects are working badly for you. However, your birth horoscope shows the strongest aspects in your particular pattern and therefore what might be especially worthwhile for you to focus on.

When the number of degrees between two points in a horoscope forms an exact aspect, its energy is strongest. But if the points are a few degrees less or more than right on, the aspect still works in this orb although with decreasing strength the farther it is from being exact.

The meaning of each aspect is connected not only with musical intervals and geometric patterns but also with number symbolism. Number families relate to musical interval families and to aspect families. You are about to meet the aspect families and then individual aspects, the major and many of the minor ones. We give each aspect's symbolic meaning and harmonious expressions. Key words for each aspect appear in italics. These key words can be combined with key words for the planets joined by the aspects. These astrological "sentences" help you understand the combination's opportunities.

ASPECT FAMILIES

A. Conjunction 360° circle divided by 1.

B. 2-Series, *Hard* or *Challenging* Aspects ½, ¼, ⅛ of the circle.

C. 3-Series, *Soft* or *Flowing* Aspects ⅓, ⅙, ⅑ of the circle.

D. 12-Series Aspects $\frac{1}{12}$ and $\frac{5}{12}$ of the circle.

E. 5-Series Aspects ⅕ and ⅖ of the circle.

F. 7-Series Aspects $\frac{1}{7}$, $\frac{2}{7}$, $\frac{3}{7}$ of the circle.

G. Unaspects Divisions of the circle that are not small whole numbers.

A. CONJUNCTION ☌ 360° OR 0°

The 360° circle divided by 1 gives us 360° or 0°, two points that are together in the zodiac.

Symbolic Meaning of Conjunctions. An emphasized unit, two energies that reinforce each other and express themselves through focused, dynamic action. Ending (fulfillment) of one cycle and beginning of a new one. Union.

Harmonious Expressions of Conjunctions. I express the power, potentials, and gifts of my horoscope conjunctions: *concentrated, unified energy that both fulfills and initiates.*

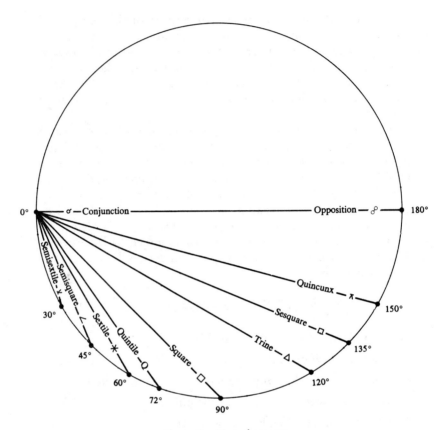

Figure 7. Map of aspects.

B. 2-SERIES OR *HARD* ASPECTS

Divide the circle by 2, 4, 8. The resulting aspects are:

opposition, 180° (360 divided by 2);

square, 90° (360 divided by 4);

semisquare, 45° (360 divided by 8);

sesquiquadrate (square and a half), 135°
(360 divided by 4 +, 360 divided by 8);

other minor aspects of this series.

The ancients simplistically divided aspects into *bad* ones and *good* ones. They considered the 2-series bad or *malefic* because these aspects challenge you to resolve quite different energy flows.

148

But, to use our musical analogy: Good counterpoint is the art of controlled dissonance.

Modern astrologers are increasingly understanding that 2-series aspects signify important good potentials of your horoscope not associated with the traditional good aspects (the 3-series to be described below).

Planets or other points in the zodiac that connect with 2-series aspects have a *dynamic* relationship to each other. They develop *consciousness* of the different qualities of their energies, a *creative tension* that is resolved by different qualities of their energies, by action and manifestation.

Opposition ☍ 180° (360° divided by 2)

Two points opposite each other in the zodiac circle form an *opposition*. They relate as a polarity, balancing each other and interacting directly.

Symbolic Meaning of Oppositions. Polarity, balance, interaction between opposites: dark-light, yin-yang, inner-outer. Midpoint in a cycle, culmination, end of waxing (increasing) phase and beginning of waning (decreasing) phase.

Harmonious Expressions of Oppositions. I express the power, potentials, and gifts of my horoscope oppositions. I am *aware* of different energies—within myself and between myself and others. I experience myself through interaction with others, resolving creative tensions into harmonies. I participate in *creative partnerships* both between myself and others and between different energies within myself. I am motivated to *manifest* myself with *dynamic action.*

Square ☐ 90° (360° divided by 4)

Two points that stand a quarter of the circle apart.

Cycle Phase. Balance point of the relationship between two energies. A turning point midway in either the waxing or waning phase. Reorientation.

Semisquare ∠ 45° (360° divided by 8)

Two points an eighth of the circle apart.

Sesquiquadrate ⬎ 135°
(360° divided by 8 and multiplied by 3)

Two points three-eighths of the circle apart, a square and a half. The semisquare and the sesquiquadrate function much like the square.

Symbolic Meaning of Squares, Semisquares, and Sesquiquadrates. Contrast between two energies, awareness of difference. Choices. Reorientation.

Harmonious Expressions of Squares, Semisquares, and Sesquiquadrates. I express the power, potentials, and gifts of my horoscope squares: I *meet challenges squarely.* I *discriminate* between possibilities, make the *right choices,* and am *motivated* to take *meaningful new directions.* I am *aware.*

C. 3-SERIES, *SOFT* ASPECTS

Divide the circle by 3, 6, 9, etc. The resulting aspects are:

> trine, 120° (360 divided by 3);
>
> sextile, 60° (360 divided by 6);
>
> novile, 40° (360 divided by 9);
>
> other minor aspects of this series.

Aspects of the 3-series are often called *flowing* or *soft*. These aspects were considered by ancient astrologers to be fortunate or *good* because they represent harmonious functioning between energies. But these *benefic* aspects lack the dynamic motivating potential of the so-called *malefic* 2-series aspects. In other words, each aspect series has bad and good potentials—it's all in how you use them!

Trine △ 120° (360° divided by 3)
Two points that stand a third of a circle apart.

Symbolic Meaning of Trines. Complementary, stable interaction between two energies. Peacefulness, perspective, natural harmony, creative expression, smooth interaction of energies.

Harmonious Expressions of Trines. I express the power, potentials, and gifts of trines: My life *flows smoothly* through the *creative cooperation* of different energies.

Sextile ✕ 60° (360° divided by 6)
Two points one-sixth of the circle apart.

Symbolic Meaning of Sextiles. Opportunities for creative perceptions and impulses, talents, constructive synthesis, insight, understanding.

Harmonious Expressions of Sextiles. I express the power, potentials, and gifts of sextiles: I see *positive opportunities,* I express my *talents* and *creative insights* constructively.

Novile N 40° (360° divided by 9)
Two points a ninth of the circle apart.

Binovile BiN 80° (360° divided by 9 and multiplied by 2)
Two points two-ninths of the circle apart.

Quadrunovile QN 160°
(360° divided by 9 and multiplied by 4)
Two points four-ninths of the circle apart.

Symbolic Meaning of Noviles, Binoviles, and Quadrunoviles. As a higher harmonic of the trine, noviles link creatively inner and outer energies. An example of this could be "the identification of self with a purpose and function related to a global or universal scheme."[2]

Harmonious Expressions of Noviles, Binoviles, and Quadrunoviles. I express the power, potentials, and gifts of noviles: My *ideas* reach *fruition* in *beautiful forms,* my *spiritual ideals* are expressed in *reality.* My *inner and outer energies* are *creatively linked.*

D. 12-SERIES ASPECTS

Semisextile ⋎ 30° (360° divided by 12)
Two points one-twelfth of the circle apart.

Quincunx or Inconjunct ⊼ 150°
(360° divided by 12 and multiplied by 5)
Two points five-twelfths of the circle apart.

Symbolic Meaning of Semisextiles and Quincunxes. Dynamic, yet potentially stable connections between quite different energies, each of which must be given its due. Focusing of vision.

Harmonious Expressions of Semisextiles and Quincunxes. I express the power, potentials, and gifts of the 12-series aspects: I am *aware* of and give *appropriate attention* to *contrasting energies* in my life so that *each functions effectively.*

E. 5-SERIES ASPECTS

Quintile Q 72° (360° divided by 5)

Two points one-fifth of the circle apart.

Biquintile BiQ 144° (360° divided by 5 and multiplied by 2)

Two points two-fifths of the circle apart.

Symbolic Meaning of Quintiles and Biquintiles. Manifesting visions. Imagination links dynamically with understanding. Old techniques link with new impulse. Creativity, fulfillment of personal potential, transformation.

Harmonious Expressions of Quintiles and Biquintiles. I express the power, potentials, and gifts of the 5-series aspects: My *imagination* links with *understanding.* I manifest visions creatively, I fulfill my potential harmoniously. I *transform.*

F. 7-SERIES ASPECTS

Septile S 51° 26′ (360° divided by 7)

Two points one-seventh of the circle apart.

Biseptile BiS 102° 51′ (360° divided by 7 and multiplied by 2)

Two points two-sevenths of the circle apart.

Triseptile TriS 154° 18′
(360° divided by 7 and multiplied by 3)

Two points three-sevenths of the circle apart.

Symbolic Meaning of Septiles, Biseptiles, and Triseptiles. Compelling emergence of higher order, higher destiny, self-knowledge, wisdom, contemplation.

Harmonious Expressions of Septiles, Biseptiles, and Triseptiles. I express the power, potentials, and gifts of the 7-series aspects: I *tune into creative inspiration,* my *spiritual direction,* my *personal relationship* to the *whole. I sense my destiny* and my *actions serve this higher purpose.*

G. UNASPECTS

As we have seen, aspects are harmonics of the circle. The aspects that function most strongly are those which divide the 360 degrees by smaller numbers: 1, 2, 3, 4. In addition, aspects formed by dividing the circle by 5, 6, 7, 12 can also be important when they are close to exact. The harmonics of all these divisions of the circle (such as 5/12, 3/7, etc.) can have significance.

If the aspects were translated into musical tones, we could easily hear the harmonic relationship of the strongest aspects. Those that are less strong connect more in their overtones than directly.

Theoretically, any two points on the circle have a specific quality to their relationship, even if it is only in the higher overtones. What we are calling *unaspects* are the relationships between two points whose distance apart is not a simple fraction of the circle.

Symbolic Meaning of Unaspects. Energies linked by *higher overtones* in our *subconscious.*

Harmonious Expressions of Unaspects. I express the power, potentials, and gifts of all links between points in my horoscope circle. Their *connections* in the *higher overtones* are *expressed creatively* in my life.

SUMMARY

1. Astrological aspects are the angles between two planets (or other important points) in the circle of the zodiac. They can be seen as slices of the zodiac circle.

2. We could think of the zodiac as a musical octave, with the signs being the sequence of notes. An aspect is the interval between the pitches of two planets (or other important points) on the zodiac scale.

3. The combination of the musical notes of all the planets and other important points is your horoscope, a cosmic chord, the imprint you received from the music of the spheres at the time of your birth.

NOTES

1. Marcia Moore and Mark Douglas, *Astrology, the Divine Science* (York Harbor, Maine: Arcane Pub., 1971), 414.
2. Bil Tierney, *Dynamics of Aspect Analysis* (Reno, Nev.: CRCS Publications, 1980), 54.

CHAPTER 8

THE TRANSFORMING HOUSES

Every astrological house symbolizes a basic type of human experience.

DANE RUDHYAR, *The Astrological Houses*

In the cycle of the houses, the process of transformation is "brought down to earth" and becomes extremely personal, applying directly to the intimate details of our lives. Where the planets show that ego's central reference point is meant to be transformed psychologically, and the signs show the basic nature of energy transformation, the houses show us how the pattern of transformation becomes a personal path for each of us.

TIM LYONS, *Astrology Beyond Ego*

It is the moment of your birth. Your consciousness is in your baby body, which is suddenly receiving spectacular input from every sense.

You had been floating, freely, rocking in wet comfort, hearing the muffled and steady beat of your mother's heart and the swish of her blood, close sounds that surrounded you.

You had faintly seen fuzzy color changes in the dark reddish glow.

Now all your senses are sending you the same spectacular message: *You have entered a new world.*

You feel pressures, air flow, temperature changes.

Your first breath brings, deep into your lungs, the air into which you have been born. The artery door leading from the umbilical cord to your heart closes. It will not re-open. No longer will your blood be cleansed in your mother's body—now this happens through your lungs.

You are hearing, with a sudden clarity and volume, a complex blend of sounds, voices, including your own voice.

The light brightens intensely and you see a complexity of colors and contrasts.

The input of all your senses at the birth time adds up to a basic imprint, containing themes that will play out in many ways in your life.

✳

Now, instead of sensing the setting, people, and circumstances of your birth, you identify with your mythic self. Your place of birth is a focal point in the surrounding heavens. Your consciousness is a unique moment of space-time in the multidimensional consciousness of Gaia. The cosmic chord of that moment is a basic imprint on your consciousness, and, deep down, it is always sounding under the cosmic music of the present.

At this moment of your birth, your mythic self looks east and receives the strength and gifts of the zodiac sign that is just rising. You also feel, pouring into the top of your head, the energy of the sign just culminating. You look across to the sign setting on the western horizon, and also sense the sign whose energies reach you through the heart of Earth.

You see the pattern of the Sun, Moon, and planets in the zodiac and how this pattern is oriented to your place and moment of birth. You hear your cosmic chord.

✻

Your consciousness returns to the round table and you see the members of your planetary council sitting around the table in the same pattern as the sky pattern of your birth. You see that each council member does his or her particular job in the style of the zodiac territory he or she lives in, and that all are also influenced by their positions around the table in relation to each other.

In addition, each council member takes interest in one or more of the twelve major departments of the continental government (internal affairs, foreign affairs, treasury, etc.). In one way or another, all departments are covered, although the council members are more active in some departments than others.

✻

As we saw earlier, the signs of the zodiac slice the circle of your horoscope, like a pie, into twelve equal portions. But there is another twelve-slice pattern superimposed on the zodiac circle. This is the pattern of your *horoscope houses*.

The *zodiac* pattern pictures *specific sectors in the background star patterns*. In contrast, the *house* pattern pictures *how the zodiac was oriented to Earth at the time and place of your birth*. To put it another way, at a given moment the planets are in the same *zodiac* positions for any place on Earth. But this zodiac pattern is seen from a *different point of view at every place on the globe*.

For example, let us say that you were born at sunrise. The sun in your horoscope will then be on the eastern horizon in your pattern of houses. However, if you had been born at this exact moment on the other side of the earth, precisely 180 degrees of longitude from your actual birthplace, the sun would have been setting. The planetary positions in the *zodiac* would be exactly the same but what is *above* the horizon in one horoscope would be *below* the horizon in the other. It is this difference in *Earth orientation* (literally *easting*) that determines the wheel of houses. Thus, if you do not know your time of birth, your horoscope houses cannot be determined even though the positions of the planets in the zodiac can be fairly closely known simply on the basis of the date of your birth. (In the course of a day the movement of the planets in relationship to the zodiac is small enough so that they are not likely to change signs or aspects. The exception is the Moon, which moves twelve to fifteen degrees a day.)

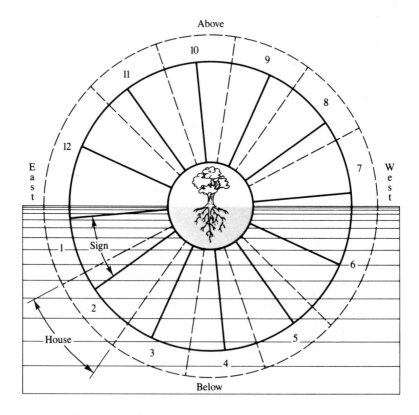

Figure 8. Variation between houses and zodiac divisions.

As described earlier, the planets refer to kinds of energies, the zodiac signs relate to the characteristic ways in which the planets passing through them express themselves, and the aspects between planets show how the different energies relate to each other.

The houses are the different areas of life experience where the energy is expressed, such as your personality, resources, communications, personal foundations, creative self-expression, working patterns, point-to-point relationships.

The houses are oriented to the horizon axis and meridian axis at your time and place of birth. These four points are called the *angles* of your horoscope. The horizon axis runs from the *Ascendant* to the *Descendant*. The Ascendant is the zodiac degree that was rising in the east when and where you were born. Your Ascendant begins your First House. The Descendant, the zodiac degree that was setting in the west when and where you were born, is the point that marks the beginning of your Seventh House and is 180 degrees from your Ascendant.

The other two angles are the *Midheaven* (usually abbreviated *M.C.* from the Latin *medium coeli*, "middle of the sky"), which is the zodiac degree that was culminating overhead, beginning your Tenth House, and the *I.C.* (Latin *imum coeli*, "bottom of the sky," which we could call the *Midearth*), which is the zodiac degree that was passing deepest through the Earth, beginning your Fourth House.

The other eight houses are distributed between these angles. (There are several ways of determining just where these intermediate house cusps begin, yielding different degrees in the zodiac.) Like the zodiac signs, the houses run counterclockwise on the horoscope wheel.

The houses can be irregular sizes, some having more degrees than others. Also, a house does not have to begin at the beginning of a sign but can start at any degree of the zodiac.

Here are the symbolic meaning and attunement for each house. Key words are given in italics. To understand how a particular house works for you, you can combine these words with those for the zodiac signs and planets in the house.

HOUSE ONE

House One begins at the eastern horizon with your Ascendant.

Symbolic Meaning.   Personality—how you interface with the world, your appearance, impression you make, your projected image.

Attunement.   I express the power, potentials, and gifts of my First House. I face the east. I sense that which is about to rise from the deeper self and see that which is just emerging, just rising. I am *oriented*. I *project my unique image* of what is rising *clearly and beautifully,* so that others see who I am and relate positively to me.

HOUSE TWO

Symbolic Meaning.   Your resources and values, as well as your attitudes toward them. These include personal possessions and income.

Attunement.   I express the power, potentials, and gifts of my Second House. I face the east and sense that which has emerged from the deep self but is still below the horizon. *I recognize my talents and resources, and develop them effectively and creatively. I manage my possessions and finances constructively and realistically, using them to bring me fulfillment.*

HOUSE THREE

Symbolic Meaning.   Your connections with your immediate environment, including neighbors and relatives (other than parents and spouse); concrete learning experiences, your usual ways of communicating and moving around your familiar surroundings.

Attunement.   I express the power, potentials, and gifts of my Third House: I am lying on my stomach on the Earth, facing down. I sense the first emergence of what I am learning from the deep self. *I learn well, think clearly, and communicate my insights effectively. My relationships to the familiar people and places in my environment are satisfying and fulfilling.*

HOUSE FOUR

House Four begins at the I.C. (imum coeli), that zodiac degree that was passing deepest through the Earth.

Symbolic Meaning.   Your foundations, where you belong, the ground that supports you, people who nourish you, the subconscious, roots of your personality, the past, security, home.

Attunement.   I express the power, potentials, and gifts of my Fourth House: I am lying on my stomach, facing down. I sense the security and peace of Earth's center. *Peace and security live in my inner self.* Wherever I am, whatever I am doing, I feel *at home. With my roots in the deep wellspring that nourishes me, my life grows and flowers.*

HOUSE FIVE

Symbolic Meaning. Your creative, procreative, recreative expressions. What you enjoy, your sense of play, your sense of the beautiful. Whatever you create, including the child in you and your own children.

Attunement. I express the power, potentials, and gifts of my Fifth House: I am facing west and sensing the *creative play* flowing from *my inner heart.* I appreciate beauty and *create beauty, purely, from the center of my heart. The child in me plays while the adult creates.* I live spontaneously, sometimes taking chances that my inner guidance knows will be won.

HOUSE SIX

Symbolic Meaning. Your connections to life-support systems that enable you to fulfill your purposes. The impact of your experiences. Your work patterns; how your vehicles of expression, including your body, function. In what ways you are a disciple and in what ways others are your disciples. How you are healed and how you heal. Services that you perform for others and their services for you.

Attunement. I express the power, potentials, and gifts of my Sixth House: I am facing west and sensing that which has just set below the horizon, the connecting point of the outer "Heavens" consciousness and my inner "Earth" self. I *function clearly and effectively* in any circumstances, learning from others and serving them, as I also *teach and receive services* from them. My *life-support systems*, my activities, and my vehicles of expression, including my body, *function smoothly and well.*

HOUSE SEVEN

House Seven begins at the western horizon with your Descendant.

Symbolic Meaning. How you experience point-to-point, "I-You" relationships, the kinds of energies you project on others and receive from others. Patterns of countering and balancing opposite energies. Energies that seem separate from yourself but that define yourself. Your experience of partnerships that serve a larger purpose.

Attunement. I express the power, potentials, and gifts of my Seventh House: I am facing west and seeing that which my outer con-. sciousness is transmitting to my inner consciousness. I am *fulfilled by the dynamic dance of energies flowing between myself and another, between the parts of myself that I identify with and the parts that seem separate. We balance and create.*

HOUSE EIGHT

Symbolic Meaning. Transformation. Inner or outer circumstances and people who bring about the ending of old patterns and the beginning of new ones. Death and rebirth, renewals, new levels of consciousness. The resources of your relationships, including income from them and mutual possessions.

Attunement. I express the power, potentials, and gifts of my Eighth House: I am facing west and seeing that which balances my experience of individuals with my experience of higher consciousness. I accept the endings in my life as they clear the way for fulfilling new beginnings. *My consciousness and life are renewed, creatively transformed. My relationships — between parts of myself and between myself and others — generate resources and power for productive accomplishment.*

HOUSE NINE

Symbolic Meaning. Your connections to broader horizons, universal patterns, understanding truth, consciousness expansion. Education, teachers, and travels that bring you higher awareness, which you help transmit to others.

Attunement. I express the power, potentials, and gifts of my Ninth House: I am lying on my back, looking up. My inner consciousness joins with that which is just emerging, overhead, from the culmination point of outer, higher, consciousness, illuminating the world below me. The universal patterns of my sky consciousness illuminate the personal patterns of my Earth consciousness, the individual features of my life. *The broader horizons I see expand my personal consciousness and bring me understanding of truths that illuminate my own life and that I can impart to others.*

HOUSE TEN

House Ten begins at the Midheaven (medium coeli) or M.C., the zodiac degree culminating overhead.

Symbolic Meaning. Your connection with society, your public activities, achievements, honor. Your vocation, performance. Your experiences of "Sky Self" wisdom, the authority figures in your life and your own role as authority.

Attunement. I express the power, potentials, and gifts of my Tenth House: I am lying on my back, looking up. I sense the pattern of my inner Earth self below me as it reflects, and is reflected by, the upper Sky self. Inner Earth self and outer Sky self unite in the flowering of my life. *I achieve my goals and perform my public roles creatively and effectively, raising my performance level for greater fulfillment.* I connect with the right use of authority, whether coming to me from others, or from myself to others.

HOUSE ELEVEN

Symbolic Meaning. Common cause with others. Your relationships to those with whom you share interests, ideals, aspirations, and creative visions.

Attunement. I express the power, potentials, and gifts of my Eleventh House: I am facing east, and seeing that which is the midpoint between my personal *I* consciousness and my transcendent consciousness. The child in me plays with others while I create with others. *I perform from my heart, beautifully, my part in the human orchestra, and the music we make together is from the center where our hearts are united.*

HOUSE TWELVE

Symbolic Meaning. Where patterns from your inner Earth consciousness manifest themselves in the outer Sky consciousness.

Attunement. I express the power, potentials, and gifts of my Twelfth House: I am facing east, and seeing that which has just risen above the horizon, into light, from my inner Earth self. I accept whatever is emerging and see how the energies of my inner Earth self integrate into those of the outer Sky self, creatively, as part of the whole. *My hidden energies manifest themselves in beautiful, fulfilling, constructive ways, in resonance with universal energies.*

SUMMARY

1. It is the *Earth orientation* (literally *easting*) that determines the wheel of houses.

2. The houses are oriented to the horizon axis and meridian axis at your time and place of birth. These four points are called the *angles* of your horoscope.

3. The houses are the different *areas of life experience* where the energy is expressed, such as your personality, resources, communications, personal foundations, creative self-expression, working patterns, point-to-point relationships.

CHAPTER 9

THE TRANSFORMING FUTURE

Our task is not to foresee events. It is to create them.

STEVEN FORREST, *The Changing Sky*

You are standing under the stars.

In your deep consciousness the sky pattern of your birth is seen, and its special cosmic chord is heard.

You consciously focus on the pattern that is now in the heavens, and you hear the cosmic music now being played.

The background pattern in the heavens is composed of the stars of deep space.

The ever-changing foreground pattern is formed by the Sun, Moon, and planets as they move through their complex interplay of cycles.

You focus on the *day and night* cycle and sense its changing phases as the sphere of the whole sky turns around you.

You shift consciousness to the *month* cycle, and see the Moon as she moves away from her encounter with the Sun, her form growing and filling out until she is a perfect round and full reflection. You see the waning of her image as she once more approaches the Sun.

You shift to *year* consciousness and watch the cycle of the seasons, starting in the darkness and deadness of winter, through increasing light and growth to the fullness of summer, followed by decreasing light, turning of energy toward the roots and the planting of seeds for the next growth cycle.

Your consciousness shifts through the slower cycles of the planets, pausing for a while in Jupiter's year, which takes twelve of the Sun's years. Your deep consciousness sees where Jupiter was in its cycle when you were born, and you look up now to locate its bright presence in the sky tonight.

You resonate with Saturn's 29-year cycle, sensing the importance of its phases as reflected in your life. You see it in the sky, Saturn of the beautiful rings, slowest of the visible planets.

Uranus erupts into your consciousness and you tune into its 84-year cycle of unexpected breakthroughs.

You dream through the 165-year cycle of Neptune, knowing that you will experience only part of it during your lifetime, seeing it as beyond ordinary reality, yet permeating consciousness with spirit and beauty.

You touch the slow rhythm of Pluto, the outermost known planet—Pluto, which takes 248 years to circle you; whose visits and phases mark major turning points in your life; whose presence is sometimes felt rumbling up from the depths, like a volcano or an earthquake—a deep transforming power bringing endings that clear the way, then bringing new beginnings.

You focus again on the present pattern of the solar system and its present cosmic chord, hearing the complex harmonies it is making with your birth cosmic chord.

Then you open the ephemeris—the book that shows you future planetary patterns—and look at the score of the future cosmic music.

✳

You and your council are playing the cosmic music. The score gives key chords for each sequence and indicates which sections of the orchestra are to be featured.

Your group improvises to this score.

Sometimes the sequences are smooth, harmonious, and easy-flowing.

Sometimes you are challenged to perform up to the music's potential.

Some measures move fast, and some slow.

Some emphasize the bass and some the treble.

Some sequences have continually changing rhythms, and some focus on a steady background beat.

You listen to the performers as they interpret the score with their own instruments and style.

Right now you are all in that magical state where you are performing as one musician.

You are in a sequence featuring the horns. The Music builds in intensity, then climaxes, and you feel the release, a rush of joy, played in inspired perfect accord.

You know from the score what sequences are coming up next, and you look forward, with enthusiasm and joy, to playing and hearing the Music.

*

You are in council, receiving reports on the state of the continent. All council members sit at their usual places around the table.

They tell you about what is happening in their territories, report on developments in their special-interest departments, and give projections into the future.

One council member makes known a situation that is building in intensity. You and he discuss what resources to call upon and how to proceed.

Another council member tells you that next month she will receive, in her home territory, the visiting ambassador of a fellow council member. They will be negotiating important issues. You and both council members discuss preparations to be made and areas to focus attention on. You envision what can be achieved during the meeting.

*

HOW DOES ASTROLOGY
FORETELL THE FUTURE?

People in all ages and places have watched the changing patterns in the heavens and seen the regularities of these cycles—the unchanging rhythm of day and night, of the Moon's waxing and waning, of the year's growth, dying down, reseeding.

Sky watchers have reckoned the longer cycles of the planets, learning well the laws underlying the dynamics of the solar system. Modern astronomy can calculate, with fine accuracy, the positions of each planet at any given moment in the past, the present, or far into the future.

In astrology we can look at the pattern of the Sun, Moon, and planets at any given time and see how this relates to the pattern at your birth. (There are also other astrological predictive methods beyond the scope of this book.) We hear how present and future cosmic music resonates with your birth cosmic chord.

These relationships between the pattern of *now* and the pattern of *then* are called *transits*. To see the potentialities of transits and to change where they are taking us, we combine the insights already gained about zodiac signs, planets, aspects, and houses with the reprogramming techniques we have learned.

For example, here's what was happening in Mary's horoscope while we were writing this book: Both transiting Saturn and transiting Uranus were passing the zodiac point in Sagittarius where Mercury was located when Mary was born. This point is in her Twelfth House.

The interplay of many factors determined just how this transit manifested itself in her life.

Some of what happened was related to conscious decisions on her part. Before the transit arrived, she had seen in the ephemeris that it was coming and visualized scenarios she liked that expressed the dynamics of this planetary encounter.

The transit worked great for the writing of the book—for many hours every day she was concentrating on, structuring (Saturn) writing (Mercury) in solitude (Twelfth House). The Uranus energy with Mercury kept emerging as breakthroughs (Uranus) in understanding (Sagittarius) what she was trying to say and how to put it (Mercury).

At the same time, the conditions, events, and people of the outer world played out themes of the transit. She heard unexpected

(Uranus) news (Mercury) from several old (Saturn) friends she hadn't been in touch with for a while.

She learned to do word processing, thus communicating (Mercury) using electronics (Uranus).

But also, her television screen kept suddenly (Uranus) going black (Saturn), thus preventing (Saturn) reception of broadcasts (Mercury). The repair man couldn't find the problem (Saturn) in the electronics (Uranus).

After the repairman's third unsuccessful visit, she said to Uranus and Saturn: "What's the big idea of teasing Mercury? Uranus— if you want to startle him, do it with a new insight! And Saturn— you are testing him quite enough while he's trying to write the book right! Both of you—lay off the TV!"

When the repairman came back for the fourth time, he fixed it. We are convinced that if she had gotten into a totally harmonious parallel universe, even that false note in the Saturn, Uranus, and Mercury passage would not have been played.

This reminds us of our friend Irwin. He saw, coming up, a Saturn-Mars transit that could be expressed in an accident if he played it wrong. Not the best day to be on the road, but it was necessary that he drive all day. When he got up in the morning, he clipped (Mars) his fingernails, toenails, hair, and beard (all Saturn). Then he drove (Mars) carefully (Saturn) all day. At the end of the day he parked in a legal (Saturn) place and was in a restaurant getting a snack. He heard a small crash outside. When someone came in to tell him, he said, "I was expecting it," and went out to find that his car had suffered only a small scratch.

He had programmed himself to avoid a big problem, but hadn't envisioned himself escaping completely.

＊

Could Irwin have escaped even this scratch to his car? Let's look at what happened to Mary's student Laura, who was going through a similar Mars-Saturn transit. She also found she had to spend the day driving, so she said to herself: "OK, I'll drive very consciously all day and I'll double my precautions. It will be all right."

As one of her precautions she had resolved to double the space between her and any car ahead of her—if she were traveling at a speed where four car lengths seems a safe distance, she would stay at least eight car lengths back.

As she went about her travels, she encountered a number of slightly sticky situations, but nothing spectacular, during most of the day. Then, in the late afternoon, she was driving along a two-lane highway, carefully keeping a more than generous space between her and the car in front of her, when suddenly she saw, coming over a hill toward her, a pick-up truck making a blind pass in her lane. The car in front of her barely had time to pull off the road, and if Laura had been only four or five car lengths back, she would have been on a small bridge with no shoulder. However, she was far enough back to pull off just before the bridge, escaping a head-on collision. The rest of the day passed without incident.

*

Here's a funny transit experience from Frances, another student. Her birth horoscope has the Moon in Scorpio in the Fourth House.

At the time of this event, she had noted in her ephemeris that Uranus was about to visit that very degree in Scorpio. A visit from one of the outer planets to your natal Moon can correspond to momentous events—after all, Uranus wouldn't be back again for eighty-four years!

So Frances started thinking what this visit could mean. She knew that both the Moon and the Fourth House can signify the mother, and she suddenly realized that her mother was planning to drive to Florida the following week—the very time that Uranus would be passing right over Frances's natal Moon position.

Uranus can mean unexpected, startling events—possibly an accident? And Scorpio is one of the symbols for death.

She called Mary up, all worried. "I'm afraid Mother will be killed on the way to Florida!"

Actually, if an accident were to happen to her mother, this is just the sort of transit one would expect, although it usually takes a combination of reinforcing planet positions to indicate such a major event.

We have seen countless examples of how transiting patterns symbolize the events that accompany them, sometimes in startling detail. But it still amazes our Western minds that these connections exist.

However, in order to keep Frances from fixating on this particular, potentially disastrous, expression of the transit, Mary said, "Remember that Uranus is the planet of the unexpected and if you are expecting something, this takes away the surprise factor! Now let's see how well I have taught you—what else can the Moon in the Fourth House mean?"

"Well," Frances said, "The Fourth House also signifies my home, and the Moon is connected with nourishing. We are having a skylight put in the kitchen next week."

"Good," Mary said, teasing her, "That settles it. Since the transit is happening in Scorpio, a water sign, you'll have an unexpected flood in your kitchen."

In the middle of the week Frances called.

"Mother left for Florida," she said. "And the men came to install the skylight. After they cut a hole in the roof, they found they were missing a part and went off to the hardware store. It was bright and sunny, but while they were gone, this thunderstorm came up out of nowhere. I was standing there, watching the rain pour into my kitchen, thinking, 'Thank heavens, Mother will be all right.'" And she was.

HOW FAR CAN WE GO?

In the beginning of this book we asked how far we can go in changing our destiny—transforming the ways our lives are manifested. Perhaps we can understand changing simple things, like being watchful as we walk along, stopping before we step off a cliff. But what if we are already over the cliff, falling?

It is even possible to get out of that one. But it takes a different order of change—something we could think of as tapping a deeper level of consciousness and will, a more all-encompassing morphic field, and resonating with that field so as to switch to a parallel universe where the outcome is something other than hitting the ground below the cliff. We call such a nonlogical change a miracle, and the greatest miracle of our times is that our world is discovering the transforming knowledge, both ancient and modern, that gives us power to reach into the heart of the fields, of the archetypes, where the real changes take place—both in our subjective consciousness and as manifested in our objective world.

Here are some ways you can work with transits or other astrological predictive methods. These techniques can also be applied to nonastrological predictive techniques.

Let us say that you, like Frances, looked in the ephemeris and saw that next month (or next year or next decade) Uranus was going to pass over the zodiac degree where the Moon was when you were born: transiting Uranus conjunct natal Moon. Let us say that this degree is located in your Fourth House and in the sign of Capricorn.

First, from our key word lists (in the appendix and chapters 7 and 8) for each of these five factors you can make different sentences that express ways this energy pattern could manifest.

Then, you can focus on the visualizations and attunements we have given for each of these factors. You can also create your own visualizations expressing the energy of this combination.

Finally, you can visualize that you are at a nodal point in the network:

✳

THE ROUNDHOUSE. **You are a train engineer. Your engine has arrived on the round lazy Susan that can turn it toward any track you choose. You experience a complete turn in the circle, pausing when each track passes in front of you. You look down the track, seeing the parallel rails leading to the horizon, getting closer and closer to each other as they get farther away, until they join at the horizon. Your inner vision sees what lies down this track— previews of coming attractions.**

Then you move to the next track and see where it leads.

When you have looked down every track and completed the circle, you make a choice and signal the roundhouse operator, who turns you toward the track you have chosen. You build up steam, put your engine in gear, and start your journey.

✳

THE TRANSFORMATIVE HOLOSCOPE. **You are sitting in the center of your holoscope. The menu on the screen reads:**

Your consciousness state
(M) Mythic Self: Consciousness of
the Metafield, the Archetypal
Realm
(H) Here-Now Self: Consciousness
Focused in this Space-Moment

You punch both M and H, which programs the holoscope to give you alternating states of consciousness, as appropriate.

The next menu reads:

```
Perspective
(F) Field, Implicate Order
(P) Particular Reality, Explicate
Order
```

You punch both F and P, which accesses both perspectives, as appropriate.

The next menu reads:

```
Space-time moment in Gaia's
consciousness
Century_____    Latitude_____
Year_____     Longitude_____
Month_____     Altitude_____
Day_____
Hour_____
Minute_____
```

You punch in the coordinates of your birth moment.

The holoscope activates the laser light beams, and you are surrounded by the multisensory holographic projection. It is so real in every detail, you seem to be there.

From the center of the skywheel, your mythic self sees the pattern of the solar system surrounding you at birth.

You hear and feel your basic cosmic chord in its original purity.

The holoscope switches consciousness state and presents you with a particular pattern, a theme that could develop from your key chord. You hear and see how variations on this theme have been, or can be, developed.

The holoscope switches to *parallel universe* mode and shows you a series of scenes that could be played on the theme it has presented. At first all the scenes are too fuzzy to see much, and the colors are out of balance. But you fix that by adjusting the focus and color controls.

In some of the parallel universes the settings, plots, and acting are so discordant and depressing that they are painful to experience. In others they are D-grade soap operas, with cheap sets, poor scripts, and miscast actors who can't get into their parts and continually try to upstage each other.

There are scenes where some of the actors magnify their parts into grandiose performances outside of the reality of the plot.

You correct all this by raising the *esthetic control* lever to the *inspired realism* setting. The holoscope shows you parallel universe scenes of higher order, in which the scripts are by a master playwright, the actors are top stars, and the settings are exquisite. These scenes warm your heart.

You access the *space-time moment in Gaia's consciousness* menu and punch in coordinates for the present.

You choose *archetypal theme* mode and hear the cosmic chord and see the cosmic pattern of the moment.

Then the holoscope presents you with a menu that reads:

Particular expression of this
pattern

You input *wolf* and *audio*. The holoscope tunes itself to the wolf morphic field and you hear the combined sounds of all the individual wolves in this field. Their music gives you a sense of the present moment beyond anything you can put into words.

Then you input *whale* and *audio* and get their special musical commentary.

You access a menu that reads:

Interactions between space-time
moments

You program the holoscope to show the interactions between the present moment and that of your birth. First the holoscope presents the archetypal themes.

Then you access the holoscope's *parallel universe* mode and are shown various scenes that could express these themes. You access only those parallel universes in which the action is being played at the holoscope's *inspired* setting—in your own life, in your family, groups, nation, and as a point in the life of Gaia.

When you have found a parallel universe you particularly like, you feed into the holoscope your own variations on it, perfecting the details until you have created your own highest and most beautiful expression of the scene. When you are happy with your creation, you touch the *transmit* key of your holoscope. Your creation is then transmitted to the cosmic central broadcast, adding its song to the human chorus, its way of expression to the human consciousness field.

You punch in a moment of the future and see its parallel universe opportunities, first just for this future moment itself and then as it resonates with your birth moment.

You punch in a moment of the past and see its parallel universe possibilities. You identify with a beautiful one and change the past. This also changes the present and the future.

The holoscope can zero in on any specifics you would like to see expressed in various parallel universes. For instance, one menu reads:

```
Life departments
(PE) Personality Expression
(R) Relationships
(CE) Creative Expressions
(PC) Public Contact
```

There is a menu for each zodiac sign, planet, house, and aspect.

Your holoscope can tie into holoscopes of any other beings or groups. It is always tuned to the holoscopic broadcasts from the human field and the fields of Gaia, the solar system, and the universe. The dynamics among all these fields create the holographic film through which particular projections of reality can be manifested. You identify with particular beautiful opportunities, choosing to live in parallel universes that express the themes to their inspired potential.

CHAPTER 10

TRANSFORMING THEMES OF OUR TIMES

It is clearly evident that most events of a widespread nature draw their causes from the enveloping heavens.
CLAUDIUS PTOLEMY, *Tetrabiblos*

The Force surrounds us and penetrates us all together. It controls your actions and obeys your commands.
OBI WAN KENOBI in *Star Wars*

✳

Your consciousness rises from Earth, at right angles to the plane of the zodiac. You travel outward, looking back to watch the orbit wheels of each planet, all centered in the hub of the Sun. Your outward flowing consciousness sees first the orbit of Mercury, the smallest wheel; then the wheels of Venus, Earth, Mars, the Asteroids, Jupiter, Saturn, Uranus, Neptune, and Pluto.

You focus on the present positions of the planets, each traveling around the Sun on the rim of its own wheel, each at its own speed. You see clearly the bright, fast-moving inner planets, those which circle the Sun in a year or less. You hear the melodies they are playing.

You also see clearly where Mars is positioned in its two-year orbit, and Jupiter in its twelve-year one.

The last planet you see clearly is Saturn, by far the slowest, taking twenty-nine years to pace deliberately around the zodiac.

✳

Then you look beyond Saturn to the largest planet wheels, those on the rim of the solar system — Uranus, Neptune, and Pluto. Your naked eye does not see the points of light marking the positions of these planets on their circling paths, but your inner vision locates them. They are moving so slowly they make Saturn look like a speeder. You see the pattern they form, and your inner ear hears the deep and strong background chords they are singing with each other, the slowly changing underlying themes of the solar system's music, played through years, decades, even centuries.

✳

THEMES OF THE OUTER PLANETS

The cycles and patterns of the outer planets, especially Saturn, Uranus, Neptune, and Pluto, indicate universal themes that are played out in specific events through linkings with each other and with the inner planets. These themes can be expressed in our personal lives; in our families, societies, nations; in our values, cultural patterns, and our way of life.

Now, through the end of this century, and for a few years into the new one, we on Earth are experiencing a highly unusual interweaving of themes symbolized by the outer planets — what phases each is acting out in the zodiac and in other cycles, and also the patterns they are forming with each other.

First we will look at the archetypal meaning of what is happening, and then we will consider some of the concrete ways in which these archetypes could be manifested, depending on which roads we take, which parallel universes we switch to.

*

When does a cycle begin? At the end of the last one. The circular snake bites its tail.

In one sense, each point in a cycle can be a new beginning, presenting a possibility of changing orbits, hopping to another parallel universe where the same cycle is manifesting itself in a different way. Yet in the phases of each cycle there are certain key points that indicate special beginnings, opportunities for making greater changes. These key points are major crossroads, where we might jump to the center of our orbit, resonate with the heart of the cosmic field, and return perhaps to a new orbit; where we can access a new order of parallel universes, make major destiny changes.

What are the key points in present and coming phases and patterns of the outer planets? We will first look at these, and how they could be manifested, both in our individual lives and in the times we are living through.

*

Then we will place this picture in the framework of a vastly longer cycle, the great age that lasts almost twenty-six thousand years and is marked by the precession of the equinoxes. In the twelve-phase nature of this metacycle we are presently living in the Age of Pisces, where we have lived for more than two thousand years, and entering the Age of Aquarius, where we will live for more than two thousand years in the future.

But before we go to Cosmic Central and look at the meaning of the Pisces-Aquarius shift, let us return to the outer planets. What opportunities are presented by the particular phase changes each of them is undergoing? What switching points are we at? What scenarios can we envision that will express these unusual themes in more fulfilling ways than we have been projecting—as individuals, as groups and nations, and as inhabitants of Earth?

*

SATURN AND URANUS. From your vantage point above the plane of the solar system you see Saturn and Uranus as close as they ever get to each other, traveling together, each in its own lane, past the same zodiac mileposts.

*

In 1988, Saturn came to meet—to conjunct—Uranus. This con-junction, with the period of close contact for the next few years, marked the beginning of, and set the keynote for, a new Saturn-Uranus relationship cycle of forty-six years, until the next conjunc-tion. What are the themes of this new beginning?

As we have seen, Saturn, taking twenty-nine years to circle the Sun, is the outermost and slowest of the visible planets. It symbol-izes our conscious forms and boundaries, our *skin*.

Uranus, in its eighty-four-year cycle, is the innermost of those outer planets discovered with the telescope, the planets beyond ordinary visibility with the naked eye. Uranus is borderline—if the environment is dark enough, it can be seen faintly by someone with superb eyesight, who knows exactly where to look.

As mentioned, Uranus and the other two outermost known planets—Neptune and Pluto—set the underlying themes of the times, below the threshold of our concrete consciousness, out of range of ordinary eyesight.

Uranus consciousness comprehends and communicates. It is like a higher octave of Mercury, which is the inner visible planet of understanding and communication. But Uranus consciousness involves more dimensions than that of Mercury, which goes on a linear path from here to there—the messenger of the gods. Uranus has been called the *enlightener*, the *great awakener*. A Uranus insight comes all at once, as a whole.

*

You are walking along a road, following where it leads you. Some-times you can see to the horizon and sometimes only a few steps ahead. When you come to a crossroad, you make choices, ponder-ing where each road might lead, exchanging information with others.

Suddenly you are raised high up to where you have a panoramic view of the whole countryside. You see where you have been and where you are going. You see the network of roads—where each one goes and what lies between them.

*

When Uranus, the innermost of the invisible planets, meets Saturn, the outermost of the visible planets, this link begins a new cycle in *manifestation* (Saturn) of *comprehensive insights* (Uranus): new understanding of the relationship between fields and that which happens in the fields; new conscious links between invisible realms and the visible world; new dynamics between Saturn, maker of forms, and Uranus, who suddenly destroys old forms, thus making way for new ones.

When these two are in tune with each other, they function like the eye. On your retina images are continually formed and registered in consciousness. At the same time the images are continually dissolving, to clear the retina for new images. An afterimage would prevent the eye from seeing what is happening now.

*

For those individuals and groups who have reflected dissonant habits of the archetypes, such Saturn-Uranus conjunctions have been disastrous: consider what went on during the last one, in 1942, with the drastic changes of political order in World War II, and the new order brought about by the breakthrough of atomic power. On the other hand, for both individuals and groups who tune into the purer archetypal themes of our collective unconscious—the archetypal heart—a Saturn-Uranus conjunction can begin a cycle of *new seeing*, of expanded consciousness, actions inspired from the invisible world that enlighten the visible one.

*

Past meetings of Saturn and Uranus have taken place at various points in the zodiac, but this one is set in a very special location. In 1988 they made the connection exactly at the end of Sagittarius and went together into Capricorn. During the year they retreated a few degrees into Sagittarius and then, still close together, reentered Capricorn, this time to stay.

The beginning of Capricorn (0°) represents the bottoming-out point in the zodiac. We know that the Sun reaches this point every year around December 21, at the *winter solstice*, when the nights are longest and the days begin to grow, when the old growth cycle has ended and the energy is deep in the Earth—in the roots and also in the seeds. At this point the new growth cycle starts—energy begins to ascend through the roots, and the seed can begin to expand.

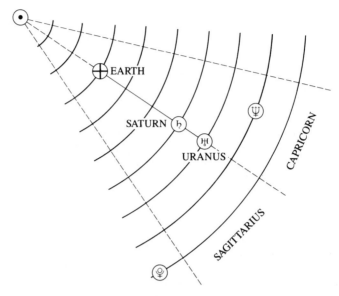

Figure 9. The outer planets entering Capricorn.

This point corresponds, in the *month cycle*, to the new moon—the "dark of the Moon" when it is joined with the Sun and invisible to our naked eyes, but beginning to wax, to grow in light.

In the *day cycle* it is the point of midnight, when the Sun has descended deepest through the Earth and begins to rise toward the dawn.

So the new Saturn-Uranus cycle begins precisely as each of these planets is bottoming out in the zodiac, manifesting the end results of their last individual cycles and focusing on the seeds of their new ones.

The structures of our lives, both individually and collectively, are tested in Capricorn. If a test is failed, further growth is cut off. But when a test is passed, the groundwork is laid for future accomplishment.

Saturn's trip through Capricorn began in 1988 and ends in 1991.

Uranus is in Capricorn from 1988 to 1996.

This combination brings spectacular opportunities for a *new beginning* (Capricorn) in *manifesting* (Saturn) our *breakthrough insights* (Uranus): how to apply our new knowledge of the universe; how to expand our consciousness and also focus on particular viewpoints; how we can express our individualities, as persons, groups, societies, and nations, yet live harmoniously as people of the Earth.

✳

You can focus on key words and images given in the appendix and previous chapters—(in this case for *Saturn, Uranus, Conjunction,* and *Capricorn*) to bring insights into how this significant new beginning can relate to your life and to the trends we are all experiencing.

✳

NEPTUNE. We have been looking at Saturn and Uranus in Capricorn. But they haven't been the sign's only outer-planet tenants. In 1984 Neptune entered Capricorn, beginning its new 165-year cycle from this point of beginning manifestation.

As we know, Neptune is the second of the three invisible planets at the frontiers of our solar system. It can be considered the higher octave of the visible inner planet Venus, goddess of beauty and love.

✳

You are seated in a garden, in the sunlight. The sky is blue and the mountains in the distance are blue and green and gray.

Next to you is a rosebush. You see that it has been cared for. The soil around it has been worked so that air and water reach its roots, and you see traces of a rich, organic fertilizer.

Its stems are healthy, but its thorns look sharp. Its new small leaves are a lighter green than its older, larger leaves.

It is in bloom and you lean over to look into the heart of an opening rose, seeing the spiraling of its petals, their almost unreal texture and color.

Then, suddenly, the rose and everything around it take on an out-of-this-world beauty. The rose glows with a special luminosity, a perfect bloom set in the perfect pattern of the rosebush, which is set in the perfect pattern of the garden and the landscape beyond. What you see moves you like a painting by a great master, and the sounds of the birds and the wind are like music by a master musician.

183

✳

The quality of Neptune beauty and love transcends that of Venus. In Neptune consciousness, beauty and love go beyond the mundane to express the spirit. When we are passionately identified with the ideal, the beauty we create is inspired.

✳

In 1989 Saturn was conjunct Neptune in Capricorn, beginning a new thirty-six-year cycle in their relationship.

The opportunity here is a *new beginning* in the *manifestation of dreams*. Other key word combinations are:

Capricorn	*Saturn*	*Conjunction*	*Neptune*
Crystalizing	wisdom	empowers	vision.
Realistic	practicality	combines with	higher states of consciousness.

You will comprehend more as you meditate on the visualizations of these four factors.

✳

In 1992 to 1993 Uranus conjuncts Neptune, still in Capricorn, beginning their new 171-year cycle of relationship. The opportunity of this pattern is a *new beginning* of *insights* joined with *inspiration*. Other key word combinations are:

Capricorn	*Uranus*	*Conjunction*	*Neptune*
Responsible	freedom	combines with	inspiration.
Organized	humanitarianism	expresses	compassion.

The last Uranus-Neptune conjunction, also in Capricorn, took place in 1822, as the Industrial Revolution was beginning.

✳

PLUTO. From your vantage point far above the solar system, you look at Neptune's wheel, encircling those of Uranus and of all the visible planets. Then you see that there is a planet wheel even beyond this, even bigger—that of Pluto, outermost known planet.

*

We have seen that Saturn, outermost of the visible planets, symbolizes individual boundaries, our forms, death and birth of consciousness in our personal self.

Pluto is the outermost of the invisible planets so far known. It symbolizes *basic transformations of form and consciousness in our superpersonal self.*

The Pluto process is the birth of consciousness of the whole, which is greater than the sum of its parts.

"Pluto," said Tim Lyons, "is potentially the complete repolarization of ego, its radical death. The god of the underworld is frightening and fertile, bringing both death and the potential for new, even transfigured life. When projected in its negative form, it becomes devastation resulting from hidden, concentrated power and wealth. In its positive, transformational form, it is a concentration and mobilization of power and individual resourcefulness from hidden reservoirs. This makes possible a true dying to old ways and a consequent refocalization and repolarization to the new."[1]

Pluto will not be in Capricorn at any time during the rest of the twentieth century, nor will it conjunct Saturn, Uranus, or Neptune. Nevertheless it has reached a key point in a very special cycle of its own.

*

You are amazed to see that the wheel of Pluto is so lopsided that part of its rim is inside Neptune's rim, and yes — your inner vision sees that Pluto is now traveling within Neptune's orbit.

*

The orbits of the planets around the Sun are not perfectly circular — they are flattened into ellipses, most of which do not deviate greatly from a circle. But Pluto is a different story. Its orbit is so flattened that the planet's distance from the Sun can range from twenty-eight billion to forty-six billion miles. In fact, when it is closest to the Sun, for a period of twenty years out of its 248-year cycle, Pluto temporarily relinquishes to Neptune the position of outermost planet. It crossed within Neptune's orbit in 1979 and will cross out of it in 1999.

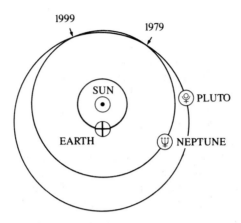

Figure 10. The intersection of Neptune's and Pluto's orbits.

This 20-year period is of major transformative significance. In the middle of it Pluto reaches its *perihelion* (closest point to the Sun—and also to the Earth's orbit), marking a key ending-beginning point in its cycle. We are now beginning a new 248-year Pluto cycle from its 1989 perihelion.

Rudhyar called this a "seed period", adding that "Germination is the crucifixion of the seed. . . . As Pluto cuts into Neptune's orbit, a process of release from the past and of impregnation by a nucleated vision of the future can symbolically be said to occur. Indeed such a period in every revolution of Pluto around the Sun is historically speaking unusually significant." He also points out that "These periods often witness a repolarization of the collective consciousness and the ideals of mankind along lines which, in one way or another, stress factors deeply rooted in human nature and thus common to at least a large section of mankind."[2]

When any planet is closest to the Sun, it is moving with its greatest speed (Kepler's second law of planetary motion). Therefore, Pluto, the background drum beat of the solar system, is at its fastest, speeding up the tempo of the whole planetary music.

There is a speeded-up quality to such periods in history. The last perihelion of Pluto (it always seems to take place in Scorpio) happened around 1741. This was a time when seed ideas were beginning to develop in science, philosophy, and politics that would bring basic transformations in outlooks and in actions. The American Revolution, a basic transformation of political institutions, began some thirty years later, and major roles were played by people born when Pluto was in Scorpio (Thomas Paine, Thomas Jefferson, John Hancock, John Jay).

The Pluto seed period before the 1740s happened around the 1490s, "the time of the Great Voyages, the 'discovery' of America by Christopher Columbus, and the beginning of the Renaissance."[3] Significant people born at that time include Martin Luther and Paracelsus (both Pluto in Scorpio), and Nostradamus (born in 1503 when Pluto had recently entered Sagittarius).

What is the significance of our current seed period of Pluto?

We have described, earlier, some of the seed ideas now developing—ideas of a whole new order of understanding our universe and of consciousness.

Rudhyar foresaw that

> what Pluto in Scorpio is likely to demand of us is that we truly and unhesitatingly plumb the depths of our common humanity. We may witness during that period a collective and compulsive kind of depth psychology at work. This could take a religious form. We might be coerced into being truly "human" by contacts with beings of other planets or realms of existence, for we only come to learn what we are when faced by what definitely and unquestionably we are not—thus also by totally alien, nonearthly entities. This could be a time when human beings experience deeply and convincingly the feeling of "community" in a planet-wide sense. It could also witness the public and global operation of occult powers, both in individuals and in the field of social and political organization—perhaps through the appearance of a powerful personage or avatar.[4]

The changes and opportunities that are now happening are unprecedented in recorded history, when put in the context of the dawning Aquarian Age, which is the subject of the next chapter.

SUMMARY

1. The cycles and patterns of the outer planets, especially Saturn, Uranus, Neptune, and Pluto, indicate universal

themes that are played out in specific events through linkings with each other and with the inner planets.

2. Now, through the end of this century, and for a few years into the new one, we on Earth are experiencing a highly unusual interweaving of themes symbolized by the outer planets.

3. A Saturn-Uranus conjunction begins a cycle of new seeing, of expanded consciousness, actions inspired from the invisible world that enlighten the visible one.

4. The 1988 Saturn-Uranus cycle began precisely as each of these planets was entering Capricorn, bottoming out in the zodiac, manifesting the end results of their individual cycles, and focusing on the seeds of their new cycles.

5. The 1989 Saturn-Neptune conjunction in Capricorn brings a *new beginning in the manifestation of dreams.*

6. The 1992 to 1993 Uranus-Neptune conjunction in Capricorn brings a *new beginning of insights joined with inspiration.*

7. The twenty-year period from 1979 to 1999 in which Pluto travels within Neptune's orbit marks a key ending-beginning point in its 248-year cycle, a seed period for the repolarization of the collective consciousness.

8. The changes and opportunities of the last decade of the twentieth century are unprecedented in recorded history when put in the context of the dawning Aquarian Age.

NOTES

1. Tim Lyons, *Astrology Beyond Ego* (Wheaton, Ill.: Quest, 1986), 81.
2. Dane Rudhyar, *Astrological Timing: The Transition to the New Age* (New York: Harper & Row, 1969), 67.
3. Ibid., 67.
4. Dane Rudhyar, *The Sun Is Also a Star* (New York: Dutton, 1975), 94–5.

CHAPTER 11

Jung viewed the Age of Pisces as a period in which Man was unconscious of his own divinity.... He saw the Age of Aquarius, however, as the time when Mankind would understand its true nature.

ALAN OKEN, *The Horoscope, the Road and Its Travelers*

Aquarius [an Air sign] is often depicted as a man with an urn of water placed upon his shoulders.... The Water Bearer signifies that Man has been created from the "waters" of life ... the water is seen as the stream of universal consciousness, inspiration, and intuition. Aquarius, therefore, distributes the riches of life through an understanding of the nature of humanity, at the same time, giving the knowledge and inspiration for the proper use of this abundance.

ALAN OKEN, *Astrology: Evolution and Revolution*

*By far the most incredible insight we may glean from the
convergence of mysticism and the new physics is that in the
coming generations our lives may be changed, radically,
awesomely. Indeed, if the implications of such a confluence
come to pass, life will be transformed into something* so
different *that its description is beyond our language.
We are on the brink of the miraculous.*

MICHAEL TALBOT, *Mysticism and the New Physics*

Let us look at the changeover from the twenty-one-hundred-year
Age of Pisces to the twenty-one-hundred-year Age of Aquarius.
When an age lasts this long, we experience the transfer of power to
the next one over a period of many years, even a century or so. The
exact point of the changeover from Pisces to Aquarius is not agreed
upon, but it is accepted that we are in the transition period—the
Aquarian light is growing, and each time a faster cycle is renewed
(such as those of the outer planets), it is increasingly tuned to the
Aquarian key.

Before we go into the significance of the Pisces-Aquarius
changeover, let us look briefly at how this cycle is indicated astro-
nomically, for that is important in understanding its meaning.

We have seen that the characteristics of the zodiac signs and the
sequence in which they follow each other constitute a symbolic
way of describing the phases of an archetypal cycle. There are two
major zodiac cycles: the *sidereal,* or *fixed,* zodiac consists of twelve
specific *star patterns (constellations)* that form the background of
the sky path of the Sun, Moon, and planets. In this zodiac Aries is
always identified with the constellation of that name. On the other
hand, the *tropical,* or *moving* zodiac places the beginning of Aries
at that point reached by the Sun at the spring equinox, no matter
which actual constellation it falls in.

These zodiacs can be seen as two different *imprints of the
archetypal cycle,* superimposed on each other and engaged in a
twenty-six-thousand-year epoch of relationship with each other.

Perhaps we can understand that when the Sun is seen in a certain area of the background sky, this sky area could become associated with—imprinted with—the phase of the yearly growth cycle
we are currently passing through (tropical zodiac).

But the zodiac of constellations also seems to make strong

imprints. We do not know why these particular constellations are stamped with the particular characteristics of the zodiac name that each bears. But the imprint is there.

The two zodiacs were synchronized, beginning a new twenty-six thousand year cycle, a little more than two thousand years ago. At that time the Sun was to be found, each spring equinox (the beginning of the *sign* Aries), at the beginning of the *constellation* Aries.

We normally think of Aries as following Pisces, because that's the direction in which the planets circle the zodiac. But the precession of the equinoxes (caused by a wobble in the Earth's polar axis) moves backwards—*retrograde*—through the zodiac. Therefore, as B.C. turned into A.D., the Sun's spring equinox position was slowly slipping back through the constellation of Pisces.

Now, two thousand years later, the Sun's position at the spring equinox is moving out of Pisces and into the constellation of Aquarius, thus imprinting each spring—each yearly renewal—with the spirit of Aquarius.

*

You are floating dreamily below the water's surface, in the womb of the great Sea Mother, surrounded by a field of lotuses. You see their roots drawing nourishment from the Earth below, their stems waving in the currents of the water.

Beyond the lotuses you see two fish, tied together, one swimming down and the other up.

You find you are floating upward toward the surface and you watch the tips of the lotus plants thrusting upward, drawn by the light of the Sun, even though it is muted under the water.

The upward swimming fish is also approaching the surface, as the downward swimming one is reaching the sea bottom.

Now . . .

The lotus tips thrust above the water surface and create floating leaves, with one side in the water and one side in the air, receiving directly the light of the Sun.

The upper fish surfaces, and its umbilical cord to the deep fish is cut, although the cord is still just as visible to your inner eyes as are the swaying lotus stems.

You, too, are born into the air and sunlight. You go ashore carrying a clay urn filled with the nourishing waters of life. You pour these waters on the Earth and watch the plants grow and the animals drink at the stream you create.

Many other people are rising out of the water, carrying urns. You fill your cups from each other's streams, and together nourish the Earth as you never could individually.

✳

The symbol for Pisces is two fish, one light and one dark, swimming in opposite directions, tied together in Neptune's sea. This represents opposing forces in the depths of unconsciousness that are nevertheless joined to each other. Subconscious instincts are polarized, like the divisions within the cell before two new cells are formed. Pisces is a sign of the water element, representing *feeling.*

To move from the water sign of Pisces to the air sign of Aquarius is a birth.

The air element represents *knowing.* The symbol for Aquarius is a person with a pitcher pouring water on the Earth. Humankind, now consciously in control of the waters of the subconscious, pours its life-giving power on the Earth so that the vital forces may flower. Thus, the Aquarian Age marks the beginning of a major cycle of renewal for humanity—and for Earth through the nurturing we give her.

Aquarius, Taurus, Leo, and Scorpio are the four fixed signs of the zodiac. These signs manifest the divine pattern, fixing it in the mortal sphere. The opposite sign to Aquarius on the zodiac wheel is Leo, representing the Sun, the outer manifestation of our center, in which we see the divine as a figure outside ourselves. Aquarius, on the other hand, portrays the divine within each person.[1]

John Jocelyn, in *Meditations on the Signs of the Zodiac,* says: "Aquarius, the Man, is the sign of signs, the synthesis of all the twelve signs of the Zodiac."[2]

The higher manifestation of Aquarius brings the importance of each person as an individual cooperatively relating to others as equals.

The need for direct experience—understanding for oneself and doing it oneself—is developing in human beings all over the world. This trend combines with increased awareness of the rights of others and allegiance to groups that function cooperatively to bring about the welfare of all.

The Aquarian Age is a time when scientific knowledge combined with intuition will be available to all people, enabling them to understand for themselves and have a far greater degree of freedom of expression than ever before. Charismatic figures of the Aquarian Age will be revered not with an atmosphere of worship, but because they are able to impart knowledge that helps individuals bring about meaningful and fulfilling experiences for themselves.

In this changeover period the validity of Piscean modes of feeling and believing are being, and will increasingly be, both challenged and complemented by the growing Aquarian need to understand. This is true for both individuals and institutions.

We are now increasingly expressing, both as individuals and as groups, the spiritual power of the archetypal human that radiates from Aquarius. Light is growing within your individual consciousness, both in left-brain understanding and in right-brain awareness. Your light is reflected in the consciousness of others, and you reflect their lights.

Old patterns of consciousness and actions are losing power as our human field is being renewed, increasingly tuned to the heart of Aquarius.

The *Pisces-Aquarius* cusp is exactly opposite the *Virgo-Leo* cusp, whose most famous symbol is the Sphinx—the face of a woman on the body of a lion. She is looking toward where the Sun rises (moving from Virgo into the Sun-ruled sign of Leo—the union of earth and fire).

This opposite cusp is the fulfillment of that union, another marriage, this time of Pisces (water; intuitive, instinctive knowledge) and Aquarius (air; conscious knowledge). This could also be seen as the birth of enlightened knowing in the human morphic field. A human brings water in an earthen container into the air and sun-fire, then pours the nourishing water on the Earth. Personal intuitive-instinctive knowledge is manifested in a particular form and then returned to Gaia-Earth. The combined flow of water from each human's jar renews Gaia, bringing flowering and fruition.

✳

Aquarian Age symbolism is not alone in pointing to the turning point we are now experiencing. More prophecies have been made about this period than any other in history!

193

"Emerging from the prophecies of many ancient cultures throughout the world are two common visions. First, the Earth must be purified in preparation for a new age. Second, the new age will be a time of peace wherein we will discovery eternity in ourselves."[3]

Many interpreters of biblical prophecies believe we are in the end times that precede the time spoken of by John in Revelation: "I saw a new heaven and a new earth, for the first heaven and the first earth were passed away"(KJV).

The ancient message of Masau, great spirit teacher of the Hopi people, is that: "We'll all be together. We will live side by side as brothers and sisters. There'll be no division. There'll be no sickness. There'll be happiness, abundance of food, everlasting life."

Mayan and Aztec prophecies marked, in 1519, the onset of nine hells, which were to last for fifty-two years each. We finished the ninth hell in 1987. The prophecy for this time was "a day of judgment beyond all comprehension. Those who survive the trial will enter the first heaven in the new, ascending order of the ages, a Golden Age of spiritual realization, planetary harmony, and for many, the attainment of conscious, eternal life."[4]

In *The Global Brain* Peter Russell said:

> The many spiritual teachers who have appeared over the last few thousand years could be compared with the first bubbles of steam that begin to appear in water as it nears its boiling point. At first, it is not hot enough for these early bubbles of steam to be sustained, and they are rapidly reabsorbed back into the water; they are but the heralds of steam. But when the boiling point is reached, there is sufficient energy for them all to fly free and the water hurriedly turns to steam. . . .
>
> The potential marriage of science and mysticism, the growth of highly efficient methods for disseminating spiritual wisdom, the burgeoning interest in inner development, and the possibility of direct transference of higher states of consciousness, are all combining to make it possible, for the first time in human history, for the wisdom of the perennial philosophy to take a firm and lasting hold.

We could be rapidly approaching a time when the "bubbles" of enlightenment would no longer be reabsorbed but would fly free as the whole of humanity begins its great transition. Suddenly everybody would become rishis, roshis, saints, and buddhas. Furthermore, this transition would be occurring at the same time that the rapid accelerations in many areas of human endeavor are pointing to a major evolutionary transition . . . we could be among the most privileged generations ever to have lived.[5]

SUMMARY

1. We are in the transition period from the Pisces to the Aquarian Age—the Aquarian light is growing.

2. To move from the water sign of Pisces to the air sign of Aquarius is a birth.

3. The higher manifestation of Aquarius brings the importance of each person as an individual cooperatively relating to others as equals.

4. The Aquarian Age is a time when scientific knowledge combined with intuition will be available to all people, enabling them to understand for themselves and have a far greater degree of freedom than ever before.

5. We are now increasingly expressing, both as individuals and as groups, the spiritual power of the archetypal human that radiates from Aquarius.

6. More prophecies have been made about this period than any other in history. Emerging from the prophecies of many ancient cultures throughout the world are two common visions: First, the earth must be purified in preparation for a new age; second, the new age will be a time of peace wherein we will discovery eternity in ourselves.

NOTES

1. White Buffalo Multimedia, *Ancient Prophecies, Future Visions* (multimedia script, Woodstock, N. Y.).
2. John Jocelyn, *Meditations on the Signs of the Zodiac* (San Antonio, Tex.: Naylor, 1966).
3. White Buffalo, *Ancient Prophecies*.
4. Ibid.
5. Peter Russell, *The Global Brain* (Los Angeles: J. P. Tarcher, Inc., 1982), 197–8.

APPENDIX

Here are a few key associations and words for the zodiac signs and planets. The words on the left can be reframed into the words on the right. See references for more sources.

♈ Aries
Symbol: Ram   Fire, Cardinal, Spring, Waxing

aggressive	action-initiating
foolhardy	pioneering
pushy	energetic
hotheaded	enthusiastic
macho	decisive
impatient	outgoing

♉ Taurus
Symbol: Bull   Earth, Fixed, Spring, Waxing

possessive	establishing
rigid	building
unyielding	grounding
stubborn	persevering
materialistic	practical

♊ Gemini
Symbol: Human Twins   Air, Mutable, Spring, Waxing

superficial	thinking
scattered	communicating
talkative	reasoning
distracted	transmitting

imitative	learning
trite	teaching

♋ Cancer
Symbol: Crab Water, Cardinal, Summer, Waning

oversensitive	nurturing
insecure	feeling
clinging	caring
attached	protecting
illogical	reflective
acquisitive	receptive

♌ Leo
Symbol: Lion Fire, Fixed, Summer, Waning

self-centered	centering
self-glorifying	loving
authoritarian	individualizing
willful	creative
attention-getting	childlike
overbearing	courageous

♍ Virgo
Symbol: Virgin Earth, Mutable, Summer, Waning

worrying	tending the seed
fault-finding	discerning
fussy	discriminating
lacking perspective	differentiating
nit-picking	analyzing

♎ Libra
Symbol: Scales Air, Cardinal, Fall, Waning

dependent on approval	relating
inconsistent	harmonizing
procrastinating	weighing
indecisive	balancing
judgmental	putting in proportion

♏ Scorpio
Symbol: Scorpion, Eagle, Phoenix   Water, Fixed, Fall, Waning

abusing power	transforming
coercive	regenerating
vindictive	renewing
destructive	healing

♐ Sagittarius
Symbol: Centaur shooting arrow into the sky
Fire, Mutable, Fall, Waning

self-righteous	understanding
deluded	far-seeing
opinionated	truth-revealing
judgmental	counseling
exaggerating	expansive

♑ Capricorn
Symbol: Goat with dolphin's tail
Earth, Cardinal, Winter, Waxing

competitive	achieving
worried	foreseeing
overstructuring	structuring
stiff	crystallizing
denying	testing
restricting	contracting

♒ Aquarius
Symbol: Human with earthen urn pouring water on the Earth
Air, Fixed, Winter, Waxing

know-it-all	comprehending
disrupting	understanding the dynamics
perverse	insightful
rebellious	innovative
unreliable	cooperating

Ӿ Pisces
Symbol: Two fish tied together and swimming in opposite directions   Water, Mutable, Winter, Waxing

escapist	imagining
impractical	dreaming
oversentimental	compassionate
illusory	inspired
self-deceiving	visionary

SUN, MOON, AND PLANETS

Here, for each of these inhabitants of the zodiac, are some key associations and words:

☉ Sun   Heart Center

egotistical	sense of self
lacking instincts	consciousness
self-conscious	self-awareness
grandiose	spirit
prideful	creative potential
authoritarian	father
self-indulgent	creative child
dictatorial	center of power

☽ Moon   Nurturer

moody	subconsciousness
oversensitive	feelings
conditioned	instinctive
smother	mother
dependent	nurtured child

☿ Mercury
Thinker and Communicator   Visible, Inner Planet

overintellectual	ideas
stuck on facts	reasoner

superficial	teacher of *what* and *how-to*
gossip	communicator

♀ Venus
Attracter Visible, Inner Planet

self-indulgence	values
dependent	attractions
cravings	desires
indifference	affections
vain	artistry

♂ Mars
Forerunner Visible, Outer Planet

aggressive	self-projector
selfish	doer
impetuous	actor
violent	penetration
hostile	drive
argumentative	growing edge

♃ Jupiter
Counsellor Visible, Outer Planet; Largest Planet

overexpansion	expansion
exaggerating	abundance
hypocritical	principles
dogmatic	ethics
self-righteous	enthusiastic
wasteful	distributor of bounty

♄ Saturn
Priest-Administrator Outermost of Visible Planets

severe	wisdom
rigid	practicality
restrained	testing, timing
guilty	structuring, architect

pessimistic	senior
problem	initiator
confined	boundaries
fearful	caution
obstacles	manifesting
challenge	conservation

♅ Uranus
Enlightener   Invisible, Outer Planet; Innermost of the Rim Planets

rebellious	originator, insight, inventor
explosive	breakthrough, unexpected,
rash	awakener, liberator, revealer
undisciplined	liberator, humanitarian, illuminator

♆ Neptune
Visionary   Invisible, Outer Planet; a Rim Planet

escapist	transcendent beauty and love
deluded	spiritual nature
unrealistic	mystical, mythic consciousness
self-pitying	compassion
deceptive	dreams
muddled	inspirational artistry
confused	ideals

♀ or ♇ Pluto
Transformer   Invisible, Outermost Known Planet on the Rim

obsessions	fundamental change
compulsions	repolarization, transcending

fanaticism	transmutation, transfiguration
cruel	renewal, regeneration, metamorphosis
annihilating	revitalization, chrysalis

Keywords for the aspects are found in chapter 7 and for the houses in chapter 8. You can put these words for zodiac signs, Sun, Moon, and planets, aspects, and houses together to make a variety of sentences describing various astrological combinations.

BIBLIOGRAPHY

Astrology

Allen, Richard Hinckley. 1963. *Star Names, Their Lore and Meaning*. New York: Dover.

Berg, Philip S. 1986. *The Star Connection*. New York: Research Centre of Kabbalah International.

Bills, Rex E. 1971. *The Rulership Book*. Richmond, VA: Macoy Pub. and Masonic Supply Co.

Bloch, Douglas and Demetra George. 1987. *Astrology for Yourself*. Berkeley, CA: Wingbow Press.

Brau, Jean-Louis, Helen Weaver, and Allan Edmands. 1977. *Larousse Encyclopedia of Astrology*. New York: McGraw-Hill.

Burt, Kathleen. 1988. *Archetypes of the Zodiac*. St. Paul, MN: Llewellyn.

Chambertin, Ilya. 1970. *Astroanalysis*. New York: Lancer Books.

de Santillana, Giorgio and Hertha von Dechend. 1983. *Hamlet's Mill*. Boston: Godine.

deVore, Nicholas, 1947. *Encyclopedia of Astrology*. New York: Philosophical Library.

Forrest, Steven. 1984. *The Inner Sky*. New York: Bantam.

Forrest, Steven. 1986. *The Changing Sky*. New York: Bantam.

Gauquelin, Michel. 1980. *Your Personality and the Planets*. Briarcliff Manor, NY: Stein and Day.

Hamaker-Zondag, Karen. 1980. *Astro-Psychology*. Wellingborough, GB: The Aquarian Press.

Hand, Robert. 1981. *Horoscope Symbols*. Rockport, MA: Para Research. (an excellent general astrology text)

———. 1976. *Planets in Transit: Cycles for Living*. Rockport, MA: Para Research.

———. 1977. *Planets in Youth: Patterns of Early Development*. Rockport, MA: Para Research.

Hickey, Isabel M. 1970. *Astrology, a Cosmic Science*. Bridgeport, CT: Altieri Press.

Hutin, Serge. 1972. *History of Astrology*. New York: Pyramid.

Jocelyn, John. 1966. *Meditations on the Signs of the Zodiac*. San Antonio, TX: Naylor.

Katzeff, Paul. 1981. *Full Moons* Secaucus, NJ: Citadel Press.

Lewi, Grant. 1986. *Your Greatest Strength*. York Beach, ME: Samuel Weiser, Inc.

Lyons, Tim. 1986. *Astrology Beyond Ego*. Weaton, IL: Quest.

Moore, Marcia and Mark Douglas. 1971. *Astrology, the Divine Science*. York Harbor, ME: Arcane Pub.

Oken, Alan. 1980. *Alan Oken's Complete Astrology*. New York: Bantam.

Orser, Mary and Rick and Glory Brightfield. 1984. *Instant Astrology*. San Diego: ACS Publications.

Pagan, Isabelle M. 1978. *Signs of the Zodiac Analyzed*. London: Theosophical Publishing House.

Rael, Leyla and Dane Rudhyar. 1980. *Astrological Aspects*. New York: ASI Publishers.

Rudhyar, Dane. 1972. *The Astrological Houses*. Garden City, NY: Doubleday.

———. 1969 *Astrological Timing*. New York: Harper Colophon.

———. 1980. *The Astrology of Transformation*. Wheaton, IL: Quest.

———. 1975. *The Sun Is Also a Star*. New York: Dutton.

Sedgwick, Philip. 1980. *The Astrology of Transcendence*. Birmingham, MI: Seek-It Publications.

Seymour, Percy. 1988. *Astrology, the Evidence of Science*. Luton, GB: Lennard Publishing.

Seymour-Smith, Martin. 1983. *The New Astrologer*. New York: Collier.

Simms, Maria Kay, 1988. *Twelve Wings of the Eagle*. San Diego: ACS Publications.

Tierney, Bil. 1983. *Dynamics of Aspect Analysis: New Perceptions in Astrology*. Reno, NV: CRCS Publications.

West, John Anthony and Jan Toonder. 1990. *The Case for Astrology*. New York: Viking-Penguin.

White Buffalo Multimedia. *Ancient Prophecies, Future Visions*. Woodstock, NY: unpublished multimedia script.

New Science, New Consciousness

Anderson-Evangelista, Anita. 1980. *Hypnosis: A Journey Into the Mind.* New York: Arco.

Achterberg, Jeanne. 1985. *Imagery in Healing: Shamanism and Modern Medicine.* Boston: New Science Library.

Bandler, Richard and John Grinder. 1982. *Reframing: Neuro-Linguistic Programming and the Transformation of Meaning.* Moab, UT: Real People Press.

Bandler, Richard. 1985. *Using Your Brain—For a Change.* Moab, UT: Real People Press.

Bennett, Hal Zina. 1986. *Inner Guides, Visions, Dreams, and Dr. Einstein.* Berkeley, CA: Celestial Arts.

———. 1987. *The Lens of Perception.* Berkeley, CA: Celestial Arts.

Benson, Herbert. 1975. *The Relaxation Response.* New York: Avon.

Bentov, Itzhak. 1977. *Stalking the Wild Pendulum: On the Mechanics of Consciousness.* New York: E. P. Dutton.

———. 1982. *The Cosmic Book: On the Mechanics of Creation.* New York: E. P. Dutton.

Bohm, David. and F. David Peat. 1987. *Science, Order, and Creativity.* New York: Bantam.

Briggs, John and F. David Peat. 1984. *Looking Glass Universe,* New York: Simon & Schuster.

Capra, Fritjof. 1975. *The Tao of Physics.* New York: Bantam Books.

De Bono, Edward. 1967. *New Think: The Use of Lateral Thinking in the Generation of New Ideas.* New York: Avon Books.

Dewey, Barbara. 1985. *The Theory of Laminated Spacetime.* Inverness, CA: Bartholomew Books.

Gaia Ltd. Staff and Norman Myers. 1984. *Gaia: An Atlas of Planet Management.* New York: Anchor Press.

Garfield, Charles A. 1984. *Peak Performance: Mental Training Techniques of the World's Greatest Athletes.* New York: Warner Books.

Gawain, Shakti. 1979. *Creative Visualization.* New York: Bantam.

Haich, Elisabeth. 1974. *Initiation.* Redway, CA: Seed Center.

Harman, Willis. 1988. *Global Mind Change, The Promise of the Last Years of the Twentieth Century.* Indianapolis: Knowledge Systems.

Heisenberg, Werner. 1971. *Physics and Philosophy: The Revolution in Modern Science.* New York: Harper.

Hoyle, Fred. 1955. *Frontiers of Astronomy.* New York: Harper.

Jung, Carl Gustav. 1967. "Synchronicity." Forward to *The I Ching or Book of Changes.* Richard Wilhelm and Cary F. Baynes, trans. Princeton, NJ: Princeton University Press.

Keyes, Ken, Jr. 1982. *The Hundredth Monkey.* Coos Bay, OR: Vision Books.

Keys, Donald. 1985. *Earth at Omega. The Passage to Planetization.* Boston: Branden Press.

Leonard, George. 1978. *The Silent Pulse: A Search for the Perfect Rhythm that Exists in Each of Us.* New York: Bantam.

Lewis, Byron A. and R. Frank Pucelik. 1982. *Magic Demystified: A Pragmatic Guide to Communication and Change* (N.L.P. Primer). Lake Oswego, OR: Metamorphous Press.

Loye, David. 1983. *The Sphinx and the Rainbow: Brain, Mind, and Future Vision.* Boston: Shambhala.

Mason, L. John. 1988. *Stress Passages: Surviving Life's Transitions Gracefully.* Berkeley, CA: Celestial Arts

Miller, Henry. 1941. *The Wisdom of the Heart.* New York: New Directions.

Peat, F. David. 1987. *Synchronicity.* New York: Bantam.

Robbins, Anthony, 1986. *Unlimited Power: The New Science of Personal Achievement.* New York: Simon & Schuster.

Russell, Peter. 1982. *The Global Brain: Speculations on the Evolutionary Leap to Planetary Consciousness.* Los Angeles: J. P. Tarcher, Inc.

Samuels, Mike and Nancy. 1975. *Seeing With the Mind's Eye: The History, Techniques and Uses of Visualization.* New York: Random House, Inc./The Bookworks.

Sheldrake, Rupert. 1988. *The Presence of the Past: Morphic Resonance and the Habits of Nature.* New York: Times Books.

Swimme, Brian. 1985. *The Universe is a Green Dragon: A Cosmic Creation Story.* Sante Fe: Bear & Co. Books.

Talbot, Michael. 1986. *Beyond the Quantum: God, Reality, Consciousness in the New Scientific Revolution.* New York: Macmillan.

Talbot, Michael. 1980. *Mysticism and the New Physics.* New York: Bantam.

Thompson, William Irving. 1987. *Gaia, A Way of Knowing: Political Implications of the New Biology.* Great Barrington, MA: Inner Traditions/Lindisfarne Press Book.

Toben, Bob and Fred Alan Wolfe. 1975. *Space-Time and Beyond: Toward an Explanation of the Unexplainable.* New York: E. P. Dutton.

Watson, Lyall. 1988. *Beyond Supernature*. New York: Bantam.

————. 1980. *Lifetide*. New York: Bantam.

————. 1973. *Supernature*. New York: Bantam.

Watzlawick, Paul. 1976. *How Real Is Real: Confusion, Disinformation, Communication*. New York: Random House.

Wilber, Ken, ed. 1982. *The Holographic Paradigm and Other Paradoxes*. Boston: Shambhala.

Wing, R. L. 1979. *The I Ching Workbook*. New York: Doubleday.

Audiotapes

Zarro, Richard A. 1987. *Futureshaping: Gaia and the Omega Point*. Woodstock, NY: Trans Tech.

————. 1987. *Futureshaping: The New Nature of the Mind and Consciousness*. Woodstock, NY: Trans Tech.

————. 1987. *Futureshaping: Visualization Programming of the Human Biocomputer*. Woodstock, NY: Trans Tech.

————. 1987. *Futureshaping: Advanced Techniques*. Woodstock, NY: Trans Tech.

————. 1987. *Futureshaping: Prosperity Programming*. Woodstock, NY: Trans Tech.

————. 1987. *Futureshaping: Lucid Dreaming and Dream Programming*. Woodstock, NY: Trans Tech.

————. 1987. *Futureshaping: Becoming A Transformer*. Woodstock, NY: Trans Tech.

Zarro, Richard A. and Mary Orser. 1988. *Change Your Destiny: Aries, Taurus, Gemini, Cancer, Leo, Virgo, Libra, Scorpio, Sagittarius, Capricorn, Aquarius, Pisces*. Woodstock, NY: Trans Tech.

RESOURCES

Audio- and videotapes on the topics in this book (see listing at end of bibliography) as well as information on workshops and other appearances by Richard A. Zarro and Mary Orser: Trans Tech, P.O. Box 489, Woodstock, NY 12498

Computer-generated astrological horoscopes, interpretations, forcasts: Astro Computing Services, P.O. Box 16430, San Diego, CA 92116-0430

Astrological software for microcomputers: Astrolabe, Box 28, Orleans MA 02653; Matrix Software, 315 Marion Ave., Big Rapids, MI 49307

Research-oriented astrological professional organization: National Council for Geocosmic Research (NCGR), 78 Hubbard Ave., Stamford, CT 06905

ABOUT THE AUTHORS

Mary Orser, M.A., has been a professional astrologer and psychologist since 1969. Her formal education was in journalism and psychology, and she has held lifelong interests in mythology, mysticism, religions, prophecy, occult traditions, and their connections to science. She has lectured and given workshops on astrology around the United States, served as a consultant to other psychologists on their patients' astrological indications, edited the magazine *Main Currents in Modern Thought,* and written four previous books on astrology.

Richard A. Zarro, R.H., has been involved with techniques for working with the subconscious mind for over twenty-five years. He has done extensive research in hypnosis and altered states of consciousness. He is founder of Futureshaping Technologies, Inc., which gives seminars to businesses in the technology of peak performance—most recently to Panasonic and the International Banking and Credit Association. An award-winning writer, poet, and artist, he has lectured at universities and colleges across the United States. He is a certified practitioner of hypnosis using Neuro-Linguistic Programming (N.L.P.), having been trained and certified by Dr. John Grinder. For more information on seminars, keynote speeches, and private consultations, or to order *Change Your Destiny* audiotapes referred to in this book, write Trans Tech, P.O. Box 489, Woodstock, NY 12498.